Cat Magick

Harness the Powers of Felines through History, Behaviors, and Familiars

Rieka Moonsong

ROCK
POINT

First published in 2023 by Rock Point,
an imprint of The Quarto Group,
142 West 36th Street, 4th Floor,
New York, NY 10018, USA
T (212) 779-4972 F (212) 779-6058
www.Quarto.com

Rock Point titles are also available at discount
for retail, wholesale, promotional, and bulk
purchase. For details, contact the Special Sales
Manager by email at specialsales@quarto.com
or by mail at The Quarto Group, Attn: Special
Sales Manager, 100 Cummings Center Suite
265D, Beverly, MA 01915 USA.

10 9 8 7 6 5 4 3 2 1

ISBN: 978-1-63106-955-0

Library of Congress Cataloging-in-
Publication Data

Names: Moonsong, Rieka, author.
Title: Cat magick : harness the powers of
felines through history,
    behaviors, and familiars / Rieka Moonsong.
Other titles: Cat magic
Description: New York, NY : Rock Point,
2023. | Includes bibliographical
    references. | Summary: "Explore the magical
qualities of your feline
    friends with Cat Magick through history,
folklore, and myths"-- Provided
    by publisher.
Identifiers: LCCN 2022061461 (print) | LCCN
2022061462 (ebook) | ISBN
    9781631069550 (hardcover) | ISBN
9780760383117 (ebook)
Subjects: LCSH: Cats--Folklore. | Cats--
Mythology. | Cats--Psychic aspects.
Classification: LCC GR725 .M66 2023 (print)
| LCC GR725 (ebook) | DDC
    398.24/529752--dc23/eng/20230213
LC record available at https://lccn.loc.
gov/2022061461
LC ebook record available at https://lccn.loc.
gov/2022061462

Publisher: Rage Kindelsperger
Creative Director: Laura Drew
Senior Art Director: Marisa Kwek
Managing Editor: Cara Donaldson
Editor: Keyla Pizarro-Hernández
Interior Design: Chin-Yee Lai
Cover Design: Marisa Kwek
Illustrations by Maggie Vandewalle: cover,
pages 4, 6, 7, 10, 15, 23, 25, 26, 33, 38, 43, 53,
55, 74, 77, 78, 81, 82, 88, 97, 103, 104, 121, 122,
127, 137, 141, 160
Printed in China

Dedication

First and foremost, this book is dedicated to my children, Hailey and Jake. You both are the light in my darkness, and I am thankful every day that I get to be your mother. This book is also dedicated to my familiar, Artemis. My furry feline companion came into my life when I least expected it, and I am extremely grateful for her. She sat with me during the countless hours while this book came into being. She gave me inspiration and, oftentimes, the words I needed to make it happen.

Contents

Prologue

It is All Hallows' Eve. The candles are aglow, lighting the room as the witch stirs her cauldron. She consults her Book of Shadows.

"The timing must be perfect," she whispers to her familiar, who casually watches from nearby. "Go and fetch me a raven's feather," she asks of the cat.

The cat jumps down, seemingly unfazed by this request, slinking away to do the witch's bidding. She is as black as the moonless night, disappearing into its darkness and shadows. She stalks with intention, pursuing with stealth to find her prize. Speaking to the raven perched high in the tree, she requests the feather and quickly returns to her witch. Magick is afoot.

This is the image that is conjured when some hear the word "familiar." While it is true that familiars come into our lives to assist us, it is often very different from the way it was once perceived.

Rieka Moonsong

Introduction

Hello there. Welcome and merry meet. If this book has found its way to you, there may be a feline familiar that is working on your behalf. Perhaps you have been curious about what kind of magick a cat can bring into your life. If you already work with feline energy, then maybe you're looking to dive a little bit deeper. Whether you currently have a cat, have been thinking about having one adopt you, or have an allergy but would still like to learn how to work with the mysterious and magickal energies that felines can bring into your life, you will find that here. Yes, you can still invoke and work with cat energy even if you do not have or cannot have one in your life. These furry and often mischievous little creatures have been proudly working their way into our hearts for several millennia. While it might be said that we domesticated cats, make no mistake, they choose to work alongside us and allow us into their lives.

As a born witch, I have always felt the magickal energies of animals. I spoke to them as a child and frequently saw animal spirits as well. I worked with them instinctually, allowing those animals to assist and guide me. Through my magickal and shamanic training, I now have a deeper understanding of what it truly means to have animal guides and a familiar.

The spirit of my familiar is currently on their fourth incarnation. They were first a Great Dane named Duchess, then a white cat named Little Bit, a Border Collie mix named Oreo, and now a tabby cat named Artemis. Being a child at the time, I was not aware that the first two incarnations were a familiar spirit, but always knew they were there to protect me. Becoming an adult, realizing what these animals were to me, and then being able to work with familiar energy is a true gift from the Universe.

Within these pages, you will learn about the history of cat worship as well as their persecution. You will learn invocations to call feline deities and spirits so that you can begin to work with them and their energies. You will gain knowledge regarding the different energies of animal messengers and guides, how and why they come into your life, and how to incorporate their power into your rituals and spell work. You will also leave with a deeper understanding of what it means to have a true familiar and how to work with them in your magickal practice. There are spells and workings included in each chapter to help you on your journey.

At the end of the book, you will find a reference section with all of the magickal tools mentioned throughout to help you better work with them in relation to cat magick. If you need to look up any of these tools, please refer to pages 138 to 146 at any time. For those who are new to magick work, note that invocations and spells have different intentions; an invocation only calls the energy to you, while a spell incorporates that energy into your magickal working.

Let's get started.

A Being Worthy of the Gods

It's not hard to see why cats display such attitude.
After all, they were once worshipped as gods.

Before diving into the magickal world of the cat, it is important that we learn the history behind it. Having some backstory gives us a better understanding of the energies we are working with. Cats have been revered and worshipped around the world, in multiple cultures and civilizations. What is it about them that calls to us? Why are they so shrouded in mystery and superstition? Why are they irrevocably tied to witches? These questions and more will be answered as we enter and explore the magickal world of the cat: feline, friend, familiar.

A LITTLE BIT OF FELINE HISTORY

It is believed that cats first came to our aid when humans began to settle in the Fertile Crescent region. The flourishing agricultural communities in the area produced large amounts of grain. Large grain stores inevitably attracted mice and, in turn, cats—the *Felis sylvestris* species to be exact—which is the wildcat that is still found today in Africa, South Asia, and Europe. It is because of the grain storage that the beautiful and mutually beneficial relationship between humans and cats came to be. The mice that were attracted to the grain were an easy source of prey for the cats, and so their hunting reduced the rodent population, effectively saving the grain. This ability was so revered that cats were brought onto ships to control the mice and then, eventually, into the home, leading to their domestication approximately twelve thousand years ago.

It is an accepted fact that cats have been worshipped by various cultures since ancient times. But why? Perhaps it is because these cultures of old not only looked to but also often relied upon animal messages. They believed that animals had their own energies and were messengers of the gods. Animals also worked alongside the gods for the benefit of humanity. These ancient people recognized the need to work with animals as well as the benefit of having them as companions. Having a relationship with an animal such as a cat was akin to having direct contact with a deity. There are myths that talk about gods and goddesses having the ability to shape-shift into animals. Two of the most famous gods that were known for shape-shifting hail from ancient Egypt.

The Egyptian culture is the first known people to actively worship the feline, going back more than three thousand years. There is evidence that states this could be as early as the First Dynasty, making it approximately 5,500 years ago. Hieroglyphics and writings in the *Book of the Dead* discuss the protective nature of cats. Also in the *Book of the Dead*, it is stated that a cat represents Ra, the Sun god, and the benefits of the Sun for life on Earth. Cats were venerated for killing venomous snakes and, through that, helping to protect the pharaoh. Feline skeletal remains and mummified cats have been found among the funerary items dating back to the Twelfth Dynasty. Feline statues of bronze, wood, and enameled pottery were quite common in the tombs and burial chambers as well. There have also been a vast number of cat cemeteries found at the archeological sites of Speos Artemidos, Bubastis, and Saqqara. Amulets in the form of a cat head were all the rage during the Eleventh Dynasty, around the twenty-first century BCE.[1]

The Great Sphinx in the Al Giza Desert is possibly one of the greatest tributes to the feline. While the head appears to be that of the pharaoh Khafre, its body is that of the lion. According to the *World Book Encyclopedia* the Great Sphinx is not only the oldest known monumental sculpture in Egypt, but also one of the most famous relics in the world. It is believed that it was created during the Old Kingdom under the reign of Khafre, circa 2558–2532 BCE.[2]

The sphinx, a mythological creature with the head of a human and the body of a lion, and sometimes depicted with the wings of an eagle, is found in both Egyptian and Greek mythology. In ancient Greece, the sphinx was a monster sent to punish the city of Thebes, devouring all those who could not answer her riddles. However, for the ancient Egyptians, the sphinx was a guardian. It was the protector of the pyramids and the punisher of the enemies of Ra. It has also been noted that the sphinx was a symbol of the pharaoh and their divine power. While it may be a mythological creature, the fact that the Egyptians chose the sphinx to represent the pharaoh's power is a testament to how they viewed feline energy.

Egyptian Feline Deities

Mafdet is the first known feline deity in ancient Egypt. She is a cat-headed deity, that of a leopard or cheetah, going back to the First Dynasty, and she would protect the pharaoh's chambers from snakes, scorpions, and evil. According to some depictions in royal tombs, she represented legal justice and punishment, and possibly fulfilled the role of hunter and executioner while accompanying the gods. She would protect the Sun god Ra from harm during his daily voyage across the sky. She would hunt by night for herself and then ensure the coming of the dawn the next day.

Sekhmet is another cat goddess of ancient Egypt. She is depicted as a lioness and a warrior goddess, and she was seen as the protector of the pharaohs as she led them into battle. If they should fall in battle, the goddess would continue to protect their spirit and see them into the afterlife. She was known as a wild goddess who would fulfill the vengeful power of the god Ra, known as the Eye of Ra. Many historical texts suggest that she would breathe fire and that the hot winds of the desert were the result of her breath. While some believe she caused plagues to serve as messengers for Ra's vengeful spirit, she was also known as a healing goddess and was called upon to ward off illness and disease.

The most widely known of the Egyptian cat deities is Bast or Bastet. She appeared from the Second Dynasty on or around the mid-thirtieth century BCE. Ruins of the goddess's temple still stand in the city of Bubastis, where annual festivals were held to honor her. She was the goddess of fertility, pregnancy, and childbirth. If a woman was having trouble conceiving, she would call upon Bast and leave her offerings. She was also the goddess of cats themselves. Like the other two feline deities, Bast was also a known protector. She was depicted fighting Apep, the evil snake enemy of Ra. Because of her connection to the Sun god, she was viewed as a solar deity; however, she was often called the "Eye of the Moon." While her original form shows her as another lioness goddess, she later took on the form of a smaller cat. She and her sister goddess, Sekhmet, became known as two aspects of the same goddess. While Sekhmet kept the lioness aspect, Bast took on the image of a smaller cat of a gentler nature. The domestic cat is seen as a living incarnation of the goddess. She protects the home, women, and children, and ensures that the mice and rats stay away.

Invocation of the Goddess Bast

If you feel called to work with Bast, you can create an altar for her with images of cats and/or lions. Caring for your own cat, volunteering at shelters with cats, or making a donation to wild feline conservation are also ways to honor the goddess. Offerings of raw meat, milk, or honey are appropriate. Use this invocation to the goddess to call upon her and her energies:

Cat goddess from the Nile
Come sit with me for a while
Honored protector Bast
Power and wisdom vast
This I ask of you
Through this working I do
Goddess, Eye of the Moon,
Help me with this boon.

TIP ⟨ Leave an offering for the cat goddess should she assist you.

WIDESPREAD CULTURES THAT
⌖ VENERATE FELINES ⌖

The Egyptians are not the only people who worshipped cats or associated felines with deity. India and China both have feline fertility goddesses. In India, she is Shashti. She was known for assisting during childbirth and was the protector of children. She was the goddess of reproduction and vegetation. Barren women or those seeking protection for their children would pray to her. She is often depicted as a motherly figure, riding a cat while nursing a babe.

In China, she is known as Li Shou. She is part of the Chinese creation myth that says in the beginning cats were appointed by the gods to oversee everything, ensuring that all things went smoothly. Li Shou was chosen to represent gods until the cats decided that running the world was of no importance to them and was, in fact, quite boring.[3]

The ancient Polish people worshipped the spirit Ovinnik, which would often come in the guise of a black cat. He was a protector of domesticated animals such as sheep and goats and would chase away negative entities as well as mischievous fae.

In Greek mythology, the goddess Hecate shape-shifted into a cat to escape the monster Typhon. She then became the protector of all cats.

The Welsh goddess Cerridwen had white cats that carried out her orders on Earth.

The Norse people worshipped the goddess Freya. She was the fierce goddess of war and death that rides into battle in a chariot pulled by two cats. Her cats were a gift from the thunder god, Thor. Viking myth did not name the cats, but they have since gained their names, Bygul and Trjegul, by a modern author. Freya was also the goddess of love, beauty, domesticity, and womanhood. She, like cats, can be seen as a dramatic set of opposites: vicious and cunning yet soft and sweet. Her cats were known to be male and it is believed that this was because it brought together her feminine energies with the cats' masculine energies to create balance.

Invocation of Freya's Battle Cats

It takes great courage to run into battle, especially when you feel smaller than the enemy, as Bygul and Trjegul may have. If you feel that you need a little extra courage, call on these two battle cats for help. Here is an invocation:

Hail! Freya's cats of battle!
For this obstacle I shall tackle
Brave and fierce I need to be
I ask that you come to me
Strength and courage you bring
A victory cry I will sing!

TIP ⦃ We use different candle colors in spell work because each color aligns with a different energy. You can use a red candle to strengthen your intentions for this invocation. Red is associated with action and courage. For a full list of candle colors and their meanings, see page 142. Please practice caution when working with candles.

Ritual for Action and Courage with Bygul and Trjegul

Use this ritual when you need to be spurred into action and lack the courage to do so.

YOU WILL NEED

- A red chime or taper candle
- Cauldron or fireproof dish
- Lighter
- Clear alcohol (Everclear burns cleanest)
- 1 teaspoon dried thyme
- 1 teaspoon dried basil
- Incense of your choice
- Small glass vial with stopper

DIRECTIONS

1. Go into your sacred space.
2. Place the red candle and the cauldron or fireproof dish on your altar.
3. Cast a circle.
4. Light the red candle, then say the Invocation of Freya's Battle Cats (see opposite page).
5. Pour a small amount (about 1 teaspoon) of the alcohol into the cauldron.
6. Sprinkle in the dried thyme and basil.
7. Using the red candle, light the ingredients in the cauldron. (Please remember to be careful when working with fire and especially with the alcohol flame.)
8. Recite the Invocation of Freya's Battle Cats two more times.
9. Let the fire in the cauldron burn out completely.
10. Light the incense and use smoke to cleanse the glass vial.
11. Once the ash in the cauldron has cooled, collect the ash, place it in the glass vial, and replace the stopper.
12. Use the red candle to drip wax onto the vial stopper to seal it.
13. Snuff out the red candle.
14. Bid farewell to Bygul and Trjegul.
15. Open the circle.

TIP ⦃ You can leave offerings to the cats and cat spirits for their assistance. Some good offerings for cats and cat spirits include: cat treats, catnip, tuna, salmon, balls of yarn on the altar, shiny objects, or milk or cream.

INDIGENOUS CULTURES AND
⸺ CAT REVERENCE ⸺

Indigenous cultures of the Americas also have their own cat deities and associations. In a pre-Incan civilization in Peru, Ai-Apec was a shape-shifting creator god known as the Mochica. He is depicted with long fangs and catlike whiskers with the wrinkled face of an old man. He had the power to shift into a tomcat. He was the protector of the Moche civilization, provided food and water, and was reported to ensure war victories.

Otorongo is the jaguar spirit that sits in the west of the Medicine Wheel of the Q'uero Incan shamans of the Andean Mountains in Peru. Coming from her place beyond the rainbow bridge, she could spark sudden change, death, and rebirth. She taught the ways of the luminous warrior and represented deep emotional healing and how to step beyond fear.

The Quechua Indians of South America made offerings to the cat spirit, Coca, to prevent temperamental flare-ups that could call down lightning to destroy crops and strike down people. Amazonian Tucano Indians believed that the roar of the jaguar called thunder. They also believed that the jaguar was the god of darkness and that the spots on a jaguar were of the stars and heavens.

The native Indigenous tribes of North America such as the Zuni and Mohave believed that the wildcat offered them hunting medicine and would bless them with a successful hunt. They kept stone effigies as one of their six hunting fetishes. The Pawnee tribe believed that the wildcat was associated with the stars and would wrap their babies in their furs to bring celestial blessings. The Hopi believed that the mountain lion was a fierce guardian of their people.

In the ancient Mexican civilizations of the Olmecs, Mayans, and Aztecs, the jaguar was worshipped as a deity. Because a jaguar has the ability to see at night, it was believed that she walked between worlds, a creature of the Earth, Moon, and stars. She represented both power and ferocity as well as wisdom and protection from evil. In the ancient city of Chichén Itzá, there is a temple dedicated to her, the Temple of the Jaguar. At his coronation, the king would walk under a procession of carved jaguars. For the Mayans, the jaguar was multifaceted and took on many guises as a deity. There was the jaguar god of terrestrial fire and war that was known as the god of the underworld and would cross souls over the veil. One of the oldest Mayan deities, God L, is associated with trade, riches, and black magick. The jaguar goddess, Ix Chel, was the goddess of midwifery and war. The water lily jaguar was considered a protector.

FELINE MYTHS, LEGENDS, AND FOLKLORE

Myths, legends, and folklore from across the globe surround the feline, too many to count. Some of the most prevalent include "touch not the cat." It was believed that misfortune would befall anyone who deliberately harmed a cat. An old sailors' tale warned against harming the ship's cat, as it would guarantee stormy seas, drownings, and even sinking. In France and Wales, there was a legend that if a girl stepped on the tail of a cat, she would have bad luck in love, engagements would be called off, or her spouse would have a wandering eye or even die. In ancient Egypt, killing a cat came with the punishment of the perpetrator's own death. Many agricultural mountain communities believed that if a farmer killed a cat, their livestock would sicken or die, and it could also bring about weak or dying crops.

Folklore and legends told of the benefit of having a cat. In some Appalachian folklore, it was said that rubbing the tail of a black cat over an eyelid stye would make it go away. In colonial America, it was believed that the house cat could predict the weather. If they spent the day looking out the window, rain was coming. If they sat with their backs to the fire, a cold front was on the way.

From Celtic mythology, and making an appearance in Shakespeare's *Macbeth*, a gray cat named Grimalkin was believed to have magickal powers, including predicting the future. In Norwegian fairy tales, cats were considered mystical beings whose eyes were portals to other worlds. And in Japanese folklore, there were the yōkai, or "supernatural cats." There are five types of yōkai in the Japanese culture:

1. The bakeneko can summon fireballs and shape-shift.
2. The neko-musume, or "cat girl," can shape-shift into a woman.
3. The kasha, a corpse-eating feline, can steal sinners' corpses from their graves and deliver them to hell.
4. The maneki-neko, or "lucky cat," is the most widely known yōkai, as it is the traditional waving cat that we see in restaurants. He brings good fortune and luck. Maneki-neko's raised paw is a sign of welcome and is often included in feng shui. That raised paw also brings money to the home and the paw held against his body guards against financial loss.
5. The nekomata is the "twin-tailed cat" that is known for being a human-eating monster once it gains its powers. Like the bakeneko, nekomata can summon fireballs and is attributed to starting large fires, killing many people.[4]

Again, many folklore stories attribute luck and good fortune to cats. There are a few "famous" lucky cats. King Charles I of England had a beloved cat that was assigned keepers to maintain its safety and

comfort. According to legend, when the cat fell ill and soon died, King Charles's luck ran out. Depending on which version you read, he either died the next day or was arrested. While not a famous lucky cat, a custom of Renaissance-era Great Britain was for house guests to kiss the family cat upon arrival to a host's home to ensure a peaceful and harmonious visit. In rural Italy, hearing a cat's sneeze meant that you would be blessed with good fortune. In southern Scotland, a strange black cat on your porch would bring the dweller good fortune. Finding a single white hair on an otherwise all-black cat was considered a good omen.

Some might say that it is no wonder that cats act the way they do today. If you were once worshipped as a god, you might have a "high and mighty, I do what I want" attitude as well. Their association with deities didn't happen by accident. These ancient cultures knew that felines were magickal creatures and were meant to be treasured. The mystical history of cats sets them up for all that is to come in the future.

Lucky Cat Invocation

Should you need a bit of luck yourself, you can call upon the mystical good fortune of the cat! Use the following invocation to call upon their lucky energy:

Cat of Luck and Cat of Fortune
Bring to me my fair portion
Please let the money flow
As I watch the wealth grow
Good luck is on the way
Holding true each and every day
With harm to none
As I ask, it shall be done.

TIP ⦃ Remember to leave an offering for the cat spirit for their assistance (see tip on page 19).

Cat Superstition and Persecution

Cats are simply little fur demons that rule our hearts.

T housands of years of worship and reverence. A rich history steeped in magick and association with the gods of old. Stories, myths, legends, and folklore all documenting the power and almost-royal station of cats. None of this could save them from the superstition and persecution that would eventually befall our feline companions as Christianity came into being.

Superstition around cats of all colors began to grow with the rise of the Church, especially during the Middle Ages. Certain cat attributes had them being associated with Satan, and because of that, they were considered evil incarnate. While all felines and most nocturnal predators such as wolves have eyes that glow due to the mirror-like structure behind their retina to promote night vision, domesticated cats are the only feline that have a vertical slitted pupil. Their larger counterparts have round pupils. This attribute aligns them with another predatory animal that is also prone to hissing when upset: the snake. Anyone who knows anything about the Bible might recall that Satan made his first appearance as a serpent in the Garden of Eden as he brought about the fall of Eve.

According to Hebrew folklore, when Lilith was banished from the Garden of Eden for refusing to be subservient to Adam, she turned into a vampire cat named El Broosha and then preyed upon newborn babies. Lilith was also known for being the mother of demons, the primordial she-demon in some ancient texts. Pope Gregory IX accused his targets (witches) of canoodling with a black cat that was actually Lucifer in disguise. In Greek mythology, Lucifer was "Light Bearer," the Morning Star, and was the masculine personification of the dawn. Diana, the Greek goddess of the hunt, magick, and witchcraft, shape-shifted into Lucifer's beloved cat in order to seduce him. Because of this Greek myth, it is easy to see how as Lucifer became Satan in the Christian Bible, witches and cats both were associated with him. During the fifth century, St. Cyril, the patriarch of Alexandria, had a vision of the Egyptian goddess Isis as a demon. Because of the cat's association with goddess energy, this aligned them with the Devil as well. Some texts state that it was believed that cats were actually humans who had committed crimes or bad deeds and were forced to return to Earth as punishment.[5] In feline historian Frances Simpson's *Book of the Cat*, "it was believed that the Devil borrowed the coat of a black cat when he wished to torment his victims."[6]

The cat is curiously absent from the Protestant Bible. Perhaps this is the reason many believe that they are evil. If cats are too evil to not be included in the Bible, they must be absolute beings of hell, right? And perhaps the cat was so revered and intertwined in ancient polytheistic cultures and with pagans, who believed that all creatures had spirits, that there could be no place for them in a more modern Christian world that believed those spirits to be evil.

Black Cats

While all colors and breeds of domestic cats have suffered, the black cat has the most history of persecution, superstition, and as being a harbinger of evil and doom. Many tales say that black cats can predict death. The dark, melanistic fur of the black cat is akin to the dark feathers of the raven and the crow, which were believed to be harbingers of death. In Ireland, it was said that if a black cat crossed one's path in the moonlight, that person would soon be a victim of an epidemic or plague. In sixteenth-century Italy, it was believed that if a black cat came to the bed of someone who was sick, they would soon die. Scottish immigrants of colonial America believed that if a black cat entered a wake, it was indicative of a family member falling ill and passing as well. One sailor superstition said that if a black cat came aboard a ship and then walked off again, that ship was doomed to sink on its next voyage. Early Christians believed that if a black cat sat upon a fresh gravesite, it meant that the Devil had possession of that soul.

Not only are black cats associated with death, but there are also many beliefs and superstitions of the black cat bringing bad luck and other ill fates. To this day, there is a widely held superstition that if a black cat crosses your path, it means you are doomed to have bad luck. It is also a bad omen if you see a black cat walking away from you. The myth of bad luck also stems from the belief that black cats are haunted because they carry the souls of the departed to hell. A folktale from Eastern Europe says that a cat yowling in the middle of the night is a warning of coming doom. Icelandic folklore speaks of a cat called the Jólakötturinn, which eats lazy children around the Yuletide season. Harrison Weir, author of *Our Cats and All About Them*, blamed static electricity stored in the cat's fur for their bad luck. Apparently, this is a peculiarity of the domestic cat. When a cat was stroked, the yielding electric sparks were believed to interfere with the spiritual or supernatural world.

Cats and Witches

It was around the time of the Middle Ages that cats became linked with witches. While ancient cultures may have appreciated the cat's ability to predict weather and possibly even one's death, the more modern world saw them as evil and in league with the Devil and, through that association, a companion of witches. Black cats in particular were seen as a friend and familiar of the witch. Their dark fur was a symbol of the night, a time when witches worked, danced naked under the Full Moon, brewed curses, and made sacrifices to their heathen gods, at least as believed by Christianity at the time. Cat's blood was supposedly used in sundry spells and cures. Healers (witches) claimed to be able to help the sick with their special brews. The church grew tired of people seeking help from witches and thus began their propaganda that their magickal powers came from the Devil.

The overall symbology of cats doomed them to their fate as witch companions and familiars. With the sleek and cunning nature of the cat, their ancient connection to goddess energy, the Moon, and magick, their ability to peer beyond the veil and be keenly aware of their environment, it is no wonder that they were tied to witches and witchcraft. Like Lilith, who refused to be domesticated, and was forced into a life of subservience, the cat is unapologetically independent. Domestic cats are small, yet fierce. Back in the day, they hunted cobras and other venomous snakes. They represent curiosity, which was frowned upon during the rise of Christianity. And as mentioned before, they are still stealthy hunters, stalking the night.

There are also significant writings and superstitions stating that witches shape-shift into cats. Perhaps this stems from the mythology of feline god shape-shifters. One such belief says that the reason a cat has nine lives is because of the witch's ability to turn into a cat eight times but on the ninth, the witch will remain a cat for the duration of her life. During the 1500s, it was believed that witches turned into cats so that they could freely roam the town and countryside, spying and wreaking havoc in their wake. It was believed they would kill babies and children while disguised as a cat, and this also afforded them the ability to run through the night to their Sabbat gatherings undetected. The stories of Lilith and the goddess Diana shifting into cats further instilled this belief.

Cats are a symbol of the wild feminine/Divine Feminine through their association with goddess energy. Being one with nature is a given for witches and important to the craft. This makes the cat a representation of natural heresy in the eyes of the church. Medieval and classical history scholar Irina Metzler believes "it is their unapologetic refusal to be tamed" that made them a symbol of heresy. In her article "Heretical Cats: Animal Symbolism in Religious Discourse," she writes about how cats toe the line between what is domesticated and what is wild. Because of their instinctual nature to hunt, they can never be truly domesticated. Those viewed as heretics by society are also considered "wild and uncontrollable," thus making cats natural heretics.[7] This, of course, innately ties them back to witches. In today's society, a woman wearing cat prints, such as leopard or tiger, is often viewed as bold, confident, and very sexual in nature. If a woman wants to feel bold and confident or even sexy, she might choose to don something with animal prints.

Invocation of the Wild Feline Feminine

Calling upon the sacred wild feminine can empower you. When this wild energy comes from the feline, it can fill you with confidence, bolster your independence and reliance on yourself, and allow you to see and feel the divine within yourself. Use this invocation for the wild feminine feline to gain access to this power and energy:

> *Feline wild and feminine*
> *Bring to me your passion*
> *Free and true to self*
> *With confident grace and stealth*
> *This I ask of you*
> *Goddess energy to imbue.*

Muggie Vandewalk

⸻ Ritual to Embrace Your Wild Feminine ⸻

Use this ritual to get in touch with and honor the wild feminine that
lives within you.

YOU WILL NEED

- A piece of cat-print clothing
  (leopard- or tiger-print scarf,
  shirt, or socks)
- Outdoor space where you
  feel comfortable
- 3 pink candles
- 3 red candles
- 3 black candles
- Holders for all candles that
  will allow them to sit safely
  in an outdoor space
- 3-5 images that mean
  "wild feminine" to you
- Lighter or matches
- Music that makes you want
  to dance and feels a bit "wild"
  (think Indigenous drumming,
  "Firebird's Child" by S. J. Tucker,
  or "Wild Woman" by Imelda
  May) and a device to play it
  on, such as your phone
- Journal and pen

DIRECTIONS

1. Wear your cat-print piece of clothing.
2. Go into your outdoor space.
3. Set up the candles in a level area where there is no concern
   of them falling over. (Use extra caution when working
   with fire in an outdoor setting. Check any local fire bans.)
4. Place any images of the wild feminine in the space on the ground.
5. Cast a circle.
6. Say the Invocation of the Wild Feline Feminine on page 32.
7. Light the candles.
8. Say the invocation a second time.
9. Begin playing the music.
10. Dance! Dance around the candles and the images.
11. Feel the energy of the wild feline feminine as it moves into
    this space, and moves and flows around you and within you.
12. Dance until the song is done. You can repeat or play another
    if you feel called to do so.

13. Walk around the candles, gazing into the fire. Fire is passion.
14. Say the invocation a third time.
15. Walk around to the images. What feelings do they evoke?
16. Sit for a moment and concentrate on your wilder nature, your passions, your inner fire, and the feelings that arise from the wild feminine images.
17. Make notes in your journal about how you are feeling.
18. Snuff out the candles.
19. Open the circle.
20. Please remember to pick up after yourself if you venture out into a park or wild space. Leave no trace rules apply here!

TIP: Offerings to the wild feline after the working is completely appropriate (see tip on page 19 for offerings). Remember that wearing something with an animal-print pattern can also help you connect with the wild feline feminine.

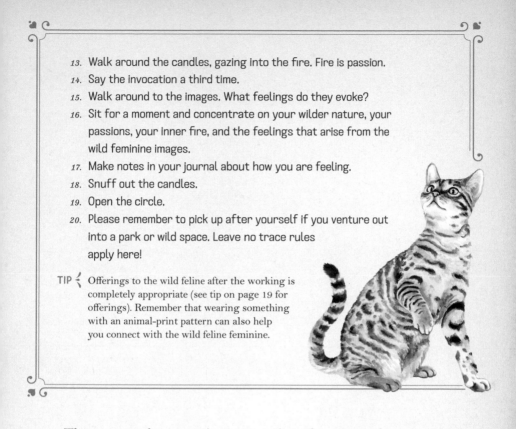

The more modern negative connotation of women and cats is the "crazy cat lady" moniker. This has become a cultural archetype that depicts a single woman, usually of middle age or elderly, with multiple cats. They are known to be spinsters, possibly hermits, and a bit kooky by the standards of society. While it is sometimes affectionately embraced, it is often a label used to describe outcasts or those on the fringe of society who happen to have multiple feline companions. Some stories tell of animal hoarders in squalor conditions. There are even urban legends in which the "crazy cat lady" dies alone in her home and her many cats begin to eat her. Cat ladies appear in much of pop culture, including some of the more popular shows such as *The Simpsons, CSI: Crime Scene Investigation*, an appearance on *Saturday Night Live* portrayed by Dana Carvey, and the psychological horror adventure game *Cat Lady* (2012) by Remigiusz Michalski. However, there is now a National Cat Lady Day, which is celebrated on April 19, and CatCon, with seminars that have been previously hosted by actors Mayim Bialik (*Blossom*) and Ian Somerhalder (*Vampire Diaries*) to help debunk the crazy spinster myth.[8]

Cat Persecution

When Pope Gregory IX issued the public decree "Vox in Rama" in 1233, it officially linked cats to witches. Because cats were associated with witches, they too suffered persecution. This was rumored to be a response to satanic cults in Germany that depicted black cats as part of their worship. This anti-feline prejudice swept through the Church and society, resulting in mass executions of cats. They were reportedly burned and hurled from bell towers. From the fifteenth to the eighteenth century, countless women were accused of being witches and thus killed. This was often simply because they owned a cat. The cats were frequently killed alongside their owner. After a woman was condemned as a murderer by witchcraft in seventeenth-century France, she was hung in a cage over a fire and fourteen cats were made to share the same fate. An old legend says that a cat can steal a baby's breath. In 1791 in Plymouth, England, a jury found a cat guilty of homicide under these circumstances. The cat was put to death.

The belief that witches shape-shifted into cats made its way across the Atlantic with the early American settlers. This belief held firm and was used to tie women to witchcraft during the Salem witch hunts and trials. "Cat scratch fever" is a very real thing and I'm not talking about the song by Ted Nugent. It is an infection caused by the *Bartonella henselae* bacteria that can occur after a person is bitten or scratched by a cat. Without modern-day knowledge of bacteria, infections were often seen as evil spirits that had taken over the body. When a person fell ill after having been in contact with or scratched by a cat, the cat was put to death if it could be found, because it was believed that it was harboring malevolent spirits within and transferring them to people.

The pagan Sabbat of Samhain (pronounced sow-in) is a known holy day for witches. Because of this, cats, and black cats in particular, were linked to All Hallows' Eve, and, later, Halloween. Black cats were often maimed, tortured, and killed on or around Halloween because it was believed they were Satan coming to walk among us.

While views have changed since the Middle Ages, there are still some superstitions surrounding black cats. Our modern Halloween decor still features them as a prominent symbol for the holiday. This is probably because cats will forever be linked to witches and witchcraft. Witchy social media pages share pictures of feline friends and/or familiars and are some of the most vocal advocates for black cats. Today's witches embrace the stereotype and relish in the bond they share with their cat. We embrace it not to go against the once-held beliefs of the Church, but because like the ancient Egyptians, we recognize that cats are truly magickal beings. They are our guides and our familiars.

Cat Messengers, Guides, and Familiars

Whether a messenger, guide, or familiar, if a cat graces us with their presence, we should indeed feel honored and pay close attention to what they have to say.

Animals are known messengers of Spirit and the gods. Cats are no exception. They can and will come into our lives when we need them to deliver those messages and help guide us. Cats are regarded as powerful animal guides. This can be as a visitor or messenger, a pet, or a familiar. What is the difference between the three and how can you distinguish whether a cat truly is your familiar? I will break down the definitions of each in the following sections.

ANIMAL MESSENGER

An animal messenger is an animal that comes to a person to specifically deliver a message from their higher self, the Universe, Spirit, their guides, their ancestors, or a deity. We do not seek these animals out; instead, they seek us out.

These messengers can come in corporeal form, such as seeing a rabbit or deer on your hike or an owl in the tree in your backyard. Animal messengers can also come in spirit form in a dream or possibly even just being seen through one's third eye. They are merely a visitor sent to you with a message. They may be there for a minute or even a few days depending on how long it takes you to acknowledge the message or if the message is of a more complex nature.

There have been stories of stray cats showing up on someone's porch and just hanging out for a few days and then leaving again, after which the person comes to some realization or manages to avoid a catastrophe. While some may interpret this as simply a stray animal passing through or a series of coincidences, it is often more than that. If a cat suddenly just shows up, or you find yourself dreaming about one, pay close attention because they are there to deliver a message. You can ask them to deliver the message in a way that you can understand. You might be able to simply look at the symbolism of the cat to obtain your message or you might need to dig a little deeper and really listen to what they are trying to convey to you.

Oftentimes, a cat showing up is a reflection of what we need in our life, such as independence and freedom to be ourselves. The natural grace and balance of a cat can signify that we might need an activity in our life, such as taking a dance class. Cats can also be associated with darkness. Taking this into consideration, they could be there to deliver the message that we are in need of shadow work and that we need to become familiar and at ease in the darkness diving into your subconscious to find the aspects of yourself that you (or society) are uncomfortable with and have subsequently hidden away. This can include traumas or anything about yourself that you deem undesirable. By engaging in shadow work, you are actively bringing these hidden parts of yourself to the forefront so that you can begin to accept them as part of your whole being. Cats are as comfortable in the shadows as they are napping in the sunshine, so they could be trying to convey the need for balance in our life.

ANIMAL GUIDE

An animal guide is an animal that comes into one's life as a teacher, to offer guidance, support, protection, power, and wisdom, and to deliver messages. They have a personal relationship with the individual.

Like messengers, animal guides can also be in corporeal form or reside only in the astral or Spirit realm. Animal guides stay for long periods of time, sometimes for one's entire life. Animal guides are often referred to as spirit animals or totems in some cultures. They will simply be called animal guides here out of respect for other cultures and to avoid cultural appropriation.

Cats as animal guides are powerful allies, especially for witches, who are able to recognize the significance of having one in their life. They can lend magick and support, help heal, and, of course, guide and teach. Our cat guides remind us to have a spirit of adventure and the curiosity and courage to explore the unknown or unconscious. A feline guide will help you create healthy boundaries and be independent and self-sufficient. They teach what it means to live in balance with social time and personal time. Cat guides remind us that we can search out our inner truths and connect with our mystical selves without sacrificing the connections within our natural environment. They help us realize that it is not only okay to embrace our wilder nature and the need for freedom, but also that it is imperative to our overall health and wellness.[9]

How do you recognize an animal guide? An animal guide is often an animal that you feel deeply connected to; sometimes it is your favorite animal. Do you feel a special bond with horses or have you always loved wolves? Do butterflies constantly land on you? Maybe you see a deer every time you are out hiking. Do you often dream of a particular animal? If you notice these things about an animal, wild or domestic, chances are that they are a guide for you.

So how do you know whether a cat is your animal guide? Simply put, you will feel it and the cat will show you. If you have multiple cats, there may be one that you are closer to. Or maybe you have a dog and a cat, and while you love your dog, the bond you share with your cat feels different, deeper. Your family or friends might notice a connection between you and your cat where they know the cat is definitely your cat. In these instances, it is often your cat that makes it known because they are particularly affectionate with their person and will sometimes even act hostile to other members of the family that they do not connect with.

You might notice your feline looking at you in a certain way or even staring at you. This could be their way of showing you they love you or, more than likely, they are trying to convey a message to you. You might also notice that after a staring contest with your feline, or while having them in your lap, you suddenly have an idea or a thought pop into your head. Inspiration might strike, or suddenly something that you couldn't puzzle out becomes instantly clear.

This is your cat guide helping you. They are delivering messages and showing you the way. In turn, it is possible for you to ask your feline guide for help. Ask them if there is a message you need to hear. Ask them for guidance. While some might say that cats only serve themselves and have us serve them, the cats that show up as guides in our lives are here to assist us on our journey, so let them. Be still, be open, and listen.

If you are still unsure whether you have a feline animal guide, there is a simple way to reveal it, using the ritual on the following page. If you do not have a pet cat, never fear because you still might have a feline as a guide.

Ritual to Call Your Feline Guide to You

Do this ritual to establish whether you have a feline guide or not.

YOU WILL NEED

- A cat-shaped candle (cat candle) or plain black candle
- Lighter or matches

TIP ‹ If you can find a cat candle, it might facilitate a quicker response or an answer to this working. They can typically be found online or in local occult/metaphysical stores. Please note that the color of the cat candle is not important to this working. If you cannot find a cat candle, then I suggest using a black candle in its place because this color is often associated with magick.

DIRECTIONS

1. Place the candle on your altar or in a personal sacred space.
2. Cast a circle.
3. Light the candle.
4. Use the Invocation of the Goddess Bast on page 16. (If you are not comfortable working with a deity or it is not part of your practice, this step can be skipped.)
5. Watch the flame of the candle. If using a cat candle, take note of how the light shifts over the shape of it as the flame flickers.
6. When ready, chant the following three times:

> *Feline guide*
> *If you're truly mine*
> *Make yourself known*
> *So our bond can grow.*

7. Continue to watch the flame of the candle.
8. Take note if your cat enters the room or if you see one in your mind's eye.

9. If nothing shows up for you during this working, let the candle burn another ten minutes, then snuff it out. To continue the working, relight and burn the candle for the next two nights (a total of three nights). Use the chant each time. (Note: Use caution when working with candles, ensuring they are completely out each time.)
10. If you invoked Bast, thank her and bid farewell.
11. Open the circle.

Pay attention to your dreams over the next few nights to see whether a cat makes an appearance. If any of the candle remains, leave it on your altar until you are certain of the working's outcome, and then dispose of it.

ANIMAL FAMILIAR

An animal familiar is a spiritual being or entity that makes a pact with a witch to assist in their magickal workings, to lend support, power, and companionship. They can assume many forms, but animals are the most common.

Some dictionaries today still have negative definitions of a familiar spirit and define them as evil or demons. This shows that while some things are progressing where witches are concerned, long-held beliefs can be hard to break. While they are spirits or entities, they are not evil or demons, especially in the biblical sense. That is a completely different energy altogether.

If you are one of the fortunate who has a true familiar, you know that it is a bond like no other. It goes beyond that of a cherished pet and beyond the connection that you have with an animal guide.

While familiars are also guides, it is important to remember that not all guides are familiars, just like a beloved pet, even a cat, may not be your familiar.

Familiars choose the individual that they work with and they can also choose their form. While witches report having a dog, rat, snake or other reptile, or even a bird as a familiar, it would seem that the most common choice is the cat. It is believed that the energetic makeup of the feline is more accepting of the familiar spirit's magick and overall energy. It is also common to have a familiar spirit that will come back to you in another form—reincarnation, so to speak. While the familiar spirit does not die when its animal form passes over the Rainbow Bridge, it is released and may choose to return to you.

Having a familiar is a true gift. When that familiar comes in the form of a cat, it is a unique and extremely magickal experience. Maybe this is because a cat is a magickal being in its own right. As we already have learned, the ancients were aware of the special brand of magick that cats possess. When you combine the natural energies of the feline with those of a familiar spirit, it is remarkable. They sit in circle with us, lend us their power for ritual and spell work, serve as protectors and guardians, can act as an anchor in this realm when we travel in the astral world, and so much more. They do all of this and still can take on the role of guide and messenger as well as cuddle with us in the evening.

So how can you recognize a familiar? How can you be certain that the adorable ball of fur curled in your lap is a powerful supernatural being? Again, it is a bond like no other. If you have other pets, take a moment to connect with their energies and feel that bond. If you have an animal guide, reach out and feel that connection, its power and how it responds to you. Now, take in the energy of your suspected familiar. How is it different from the others? Some describe this bond as being similar to a soul mate connection. Imagine being at a pet store having an adoption event and you wander over to a kennel full of kittens. One meets your eyes and it feels like an, "OH! There you are!" moment. That is what it feels like to connect with your familiar. You sense their power, even as a kitten. You know that they have chosen you.

If you are still uncertain as to whether or not your cat is your familiar, there are several things you can do. One would be to consult a pendulum if you are used to working with one. Start by asking whether you have a familiar, then, if the answer is affirmative, hold the pendulum over the cat in question and ask whether they are the familiar spirit that has chosen you. If yes, you have your answer. If not, check any other animals that you might have. If the answer is no, then your familiar has either not taken a corporeal form yet or they never intend to, but will assist you from the astral or Spirit realm. Remember, when working with a pendulum, figure out for yourself which movement of the pendulum means "no" and which movement means "yes" before asking it for guidance, as each movement can mean different answers for everyone.

Another way to reveal whether you have a feline familiar is by performing a little bit of spell work. This will also help facilitate contact between you and your familiar spirit. This kind of spell work is similar to the spell work that helps reveal whether your cat is your animal guide.

Ritual to Reveal Your Feline Familiar to You

Perform this ritual if you want or need to find your familiar.

- A cat candle or a plain black candle
- Lighter or matches

TIP ⚡ If you can find a cat candle, it might facilitate a quicker response or answer to this working. They can typically be found online or in local occult/metaphysical stores. Please note that the color of the cat candle is not important to this working. If you cannot find a cat candle, then I suggest using a black candle in its place, as this color is often associated with magick.

DIRECTIONS

1. Place the candle on your altar or in a personal sacred space.
2. Cast a circle.
3. Light the candle.
4. Intone the following invocation three times:

> *If it's truly meant to be*
> *And you are to work with me*
> *Oh feline familiar spirit*
> *This is my call so hear it*
> *It is time for your reveal*
> *Let the magick be our seal.*
> *So mote it be (after the third time).*

5. Continue to watch the flame of the candle.
6. Take note if your cat enters the room or if you see one in your mind's eye.
7. If nothing shows up for you during this working, let the candle burn another ten minutes, and then snuff it out. To continue the working, relight and burn for the next two nights (a total of three nights). Use the chant each time.
8. Open the circle.

TIP ⚡ Pay attention to your dreams over the next few nights to see whether a cat makes an appearance. If there are any candle remains, leave them on the altar until you're sure of the spell's outcome, and then dispose of them.

GUIDES VS. FAMILIARS

So, now that we know what guides and familiars are, and how to recognize them, how do they differ? What roles do they truly play in our lives? How can we connect with them on an energetic level? One of the main differences begins right in the very definition of what they are, not only in relation to us, but also in power and overall energetic makeup. Their roles in our lives may vary depending on what we need them to be.

As mentioned before, guides can exist in corporeal form or solely in the astral or other metaphysical planes. You could also have a pet as your guide that passes over the Rainbow Bridge and then their spirit stays with you to continue to guide you. Familiars too can exist in the physical or metaphysical plane. While a guide spirit can choose to remain with someone for the rest of their natural life, a familiar spirit can choose to reincarnate and come back again and again, even returning in their witch's next life if they are once again a spiritual person, witch, shaman, etc.

Anyone can have an animal guide—be it a cat, dog, bird, bear, wolf, lizard, dolphin, or any other animal—even if they are not aware of them. Some people even have multiple animal guides. This is especially common among magickal people. However, only witches, shamans, and other magickal people have a familiar, and they can only have one at any given time. This does not mean that if their familiar has a physical form and then passes to the beyond that another familiar will not come to take its place. There are some stories of a person having one familiar in their younger life and then a different familiar spirit in their older life. This is not the same as the familiar spirit reincarnating in a different form. It is a completely different entity altogether. This could be an example of how the energetic or magickal needs of the witch change over time and the need for a different type of power that comes with each familiar spirit.

If you have not yet established that you have a feline animal guide and/or a familiar with spell work, then it is advised that you do so before trying to truly connect or bond with them. Once the presence of a cat guide has been established, you can connect and bond with them through meditations or a Lower World shamanic journey (see pages 53-54) if they do not have a corporeal form. If the cat guide shows up as a stray cat or is a pet in your home, bond with them by taking care of them and talking to them. Speaking to them establishes that you are open to communication. Ask them questions like you might another person, such as "How was your day?" or "Tell me about what was going on in the house last night." Don't be surprised when you start getting impressions about their feelings, images that show up in your mind, or even actual words that come into your thoughts that are not your own. This is their way of speaking with you.

Even though the bond with one's familiar involves taking care of them, the bond is really forged and strengthened through magickal workings. Anytime you are working a spell or doing a ritual, have them in the room with you. If you are outside, you might be able to use a cat harness to have them with you or keep them in their pet carrier, as long as this does not distress them. It is advised to wait until the cat reaches adulthood before consciously pulling on their magick or asking them to lend it. This is just for the safety of the kitten form that is the vessel for the familiar spirit, as they are still growing and that requires a significant amount of energy. The bond with a feline familiar that exists solely on the astral plane is also established through magickal workings.

While it is more common to have a feline familiar spirit that comes to the witch in its corporeal form as a pet house cat, remember that they can also show up as a stray that comes and goes as they choose, appearing every few days, syncing with Moon cycles, or coming when magick is afoot. If this is the case, it is up to the witch to respect the boundaries that their familiar is setting. It is believed that the entities that are familiar spirits come as stray cats when it is their first time coming out of the astral or other metaphysical realms. It is an adjustment for them being in physical form and they may find it difficult to stay in one place for long periods of time. You can still bond with them in the same way, by leaving out food and water, maybe making a small shelter with a blanket, and talking to them when they are around. If they will allow it, you can let them in for a bit while you do magickal workings. However, these types of familiars will generally be more comfortable with outdoor rituals and spell work.

Animal guides and familiars that exist only in the metaphysical realm can also make appearances in the physical world. This can come in the form of stray cats showing up on your porch or even outside your workplace. How will you know whether this is more than just a stray animal? Open yourself up and feel it. Have you asked for something of your guide or familiar recently? Have you been seeking guidance or the answer to a problem or question? If yes, then this is more than likely their way of bringing that message or coming to your aid. Another possible form they may take is that of a big cat. Try making a trip to a big cat sanctuary or a local zoo if there is one in your area. There are stories of a lion or tiger coming up to the glass of their enclosure and staring intently at a person. Don't discount these types of encounters if they happen. Again, be open and listen.

The role of domestic cats in general is to clear our homes of unwanted or negative energies. Our feline guides simply serve as just that—a guide. They are here to deliver messages and teach us. A cat guide will often lead you to your spiritual or magickal life. This does not mean you cannot work with them on a magickal level. While they can lend power and support, it is not where their true abilities lie. A feline familiar spirit, however, comes into our lives to help us on our magickal journey and to fulfill our destiny as a witch. They lend us power and their own magick, melding it with ours to be able to reach into those other dimensions and access higher energies and magicks. They are protectors and guardians.

While it is common for a witch to have a pet that is also a guide or familiar, it is important to remember that the majority of them are simply pets. That does not mean that they are not wonderful companions and that we love them any less. It simply means that the animal is not in our life to serve us in a magickal way. Because cats are magickal creatures in their own right, it is still completely possible to work with their energies; it is just different from that of a guide or familiar.

It is said that the reason house cats always seem so disgruntled is because they are the perfect predator. They have everything that a tiger has—razor-sharp retracting claws, teeth that pierce, stealth and grace, incredible jumping, climbing, and pouncing ability—yet they only weigh eight pounds and we can continually pick them up to cuddle. When you think about it, you can see the truth in this. It's all there, only on a smaller scale for the felines of the house. The energies of a domestic cat and that of a big cat are similar.

Another possibility, although rare, is having a big cat as a familiar. You might be thinking, "How on Earth would I work with them?" Should you do the spell to reveal your familiar and end up with a mountain lion, have no fear. There are ways to work with these animals, it just takes a little more effort.

⸺ LOWER WORLD SHAMANIC JOURNEY ⸺

In the Andean shamanic tradition, the Lower World (not to be confused with Christian hell) is where our animal guides reside. To journey to the Lower World, I suggest that you record the following text that I have created and then play it back until you are able to journey there on your own. Drumming in the background is often found to be helpful for journey work. Set a timer for twenty to thirty minutes to bring you back.

Ritual Recording to Reveal Your
Feline Familiar Guide to You

Close your eyes and take three deep breaths, slowly inhaling and exhaling each one . . . Now imagine yourself in a large meadow. See the grasses moving in the breeze. You notice that there is a forest at the edge of the meadow. You begin to make your way to the trees and you see a path. Follow it. The path through the trees begins to descend a little until you reach a dead end at a massive tree that reaches out in all directions. You notice a large opening at the base of the tree and that the path continues into this opening. This is the entrance to the Lower World and there is a being that guards it. You ask their permission to enter. They allow you access and point to the path that continues onward. The path descends, down, down, down. It winds and spirals down into the Earth until you reach an underground stream. You instinctively lie down in the water and let it wash over you, cleansing you. You step out again on the other side and are dry. You continue on the path until you see an opening with light spilling in. When you reach the opening, you find yourself in a beautiful world with meadows, flowers, trees, and animals of all kinds. There is a bench waiting for you, so you take a seat. In the distance, you can see a feline approaching you. It is your guide and it is time to bond with them . . . You will stay here until you hear the timer calling you back. When you hear its call, travel back the way you came.

Take time to write down your experience in your journal—any messages that came through or special guidance they had to offer you. Remember that you can make this journey any time you wish to.

Big Cat Energy

Big cats can strike fear in the hearts of those that might encounter them. More often than not, they watch, ever curious. Learn how to listen to their energy. Mountain lions can even warn of dangers on the trail. No, do not fear them; listen to them.

C at magick is not limited to that of the domestic cat. The energy of the big cats is powerful and they can be wonderful allies in your spell work or rituals. It is trickier to work with this big cat energy than that of a house cat. You cannot simply bring a tiger or mountain lion into your home. Unless you can easily access a big cat sanctuary, and even then it still might prove difficult, most of this work will be done in the astral world or by calling the energy or spirit of a big cat to you.

Before you consider working with big cat energy, it is important to have an understanding of their different energies. Most of the big cats hold the essence of the Divine Feminine. There is, however, one exception to that. Mother Nature tries to achieve balance, containing both the Divine Feminine and the Divine Masculine that come together in harmony. Because of this, she gives us both masculine and feminine big cat energy to work with. The role of these magnificent creatures is similar to that of the domestic cat, and that is to keep their territories free of any negative energies. They also try to help heal the Earth.

MASCULINE LION ENERGY

The masculine energy of the big cats is held within the regal lion. Looking at images of him, it is easy to see why he is called the "king of beasts." Some believe that the masculine energies of the lion serve as a protector from unwanted visitors to our planet. His mighty roar reverberates through the layers of the Earth, sending out the signal to stay away. He symbolizes majesty, grace, leadership, strength, and courage. His vibrant yellow-gold mane is a symbol of solar energy in many ancient cultures, thus tying the lion to the Divine Masculine and the power of the Sun. Lion energy is one of warmth and vitality, drawing you in and infusing you with passion and a love of life.

If the mighty lion comes roaring into your life as a messenger, know that it is time to act. He is often delivering messages that relate to standing in your power, or taking your power back, stepping into a leadership role, the need for familial protection, or to banish any fears and have the courage to do what needs to be done. He may also be letting you know that you need to balance or tap into the Divine Masculine within you.

When the lion is your personal animal guide, he is infusing you with the energy of the leadership role. People with lion guides are those who lead with seemingly effortless grace; they are naturals when it comes to taking the helm. He walks beside his charge, helping them maintain a balance within the ranks through strong ideals and morals while taking challenges head-on. He will guide them to ways of self-expression that are humble yet steadfast.

Those who encounter the lion as their familiar will find that he lends almost limitless power to their magickal workings. He also gives his witch the ability to soak up major solar energy and be able to channel it into their spells. "Lion people" often love summer and find themselves drawn to solar or fire deities and energies. Their lion familiar will teach them how to work with those energies with respect and how to honor their own Divine Masculine power as we all hold this energy within us.

Witches and other magickal people who are graced with a lion familiar may find themselves as the leader of a coven or even a teacher of witchcraft, shamanism, or other spiritual paths. Lions have a close and intuitive alignment with their throat and crown chakras, naturally connecting them to higher universal energies and communication. As a familiar, the lion will graciously share these connections and communication skills with his chosen witch.[10]

The black cats—melanistic leopards and jaguars—are commonly called "black panthers." They hold feminine energies and are said to be spiritual leaders that help us humans raise our vibrations. Like their smaller domestic counterparts, black leopards and jaguars are also associated with witches and witchcraft. Both of these big cats are one with the night and lunar energy.

Because of the high levels of melanin that cloak their spots, both the black jaguar and the black leopard come into your life as messengers, signaling that it is time to remove the mask that you are hiding behind. The black panther also delivers the messages that it is time to face the darkness and the need for shadow work.

If the black panther is your animal guide, you will more than likely have an affinity for lunar energy and workings that revolve around the phases of the Moon. "Black panther people" typically love their alone time and tend to be night owls. As a guide, the black panther will teach their person to develop their natural psychic abilities. They can also help you unlock your sensual and sexual self.

Much like the black panther as a guide, a black panther familiar brings their witch powerful lunar magick. Those with a black panther familiar tend to be solitary witches and like to work with lunar goddesses and often dark goddess energy. Black panther familiars teach their witches not to fear the darkness that lives within all of us, and will help them fully integrate their shadow self. Since the black panther is the ultimate shape-shifter and a master of disguise, as a familiar they will bring this knowledge to their witch so that they too can cloak themselves and have the ability to move between worlds unseen. They will help increase the witch's psychic abilities as well as aid in divination or scrying spells.

Though the leopard and jaguar are the same as their melanistic counterparts, except for the genetic variance that colors them black, they do hold different energies. While they still carry that of the Divine Feminine, they bring different lessons with them.

There is a saying that "a leopard cannot change its spots," and while most apply this meaning in a negative connotation, this saying can also contain the leopard's most powerful guidance: to be unapologetically yourself. Wear your spots with pride, as there is no need to hide them. The leopard as an animal guide teaches us to trust our intuition and instincts and not to second-guess ourselves. The leopard shows their charge how to be self-reliant. As animals that can often be found in the trees and have impeccable vision, they remind us that sometimes the answer to a problem is all about changing our perception.

As a familiar, the leopard lends a great deal of strength to their witch. They are one of the smallest of the big cats and yet one of the strongest, being able to drag prey three times their body weight up into a tree. They remind the witch that the sheer force of their will and belief in themselves are what magick is all about. The leopard familiar guides the witch on their path, always reminding them of who they truly are and to have faith in their own power. Like many of the other big cats, leopards have excellent night vision and will bless the witch with the ability to see into the darkness, which includes exceptional divination skills.

Snow leopards reside in the peaks of the Himalaya mountains. As an animal guide, these cats will teach you the art of elusiveness and being able to hide in plain sight when necessary. Because of the inhospitable environment in which they live, they can also teach us a lot about what it means to be able to survive when we don't think that it is possible.

The snow leopard is revered by the Nepalese people as a keeper of ancient wisdom, and so to have one as your familiar, you too will be blessed with this ancient wisdom and knowledge. Snow leopard familiars give us resilience and the ability to conserve energies. They will give a witch the power of inner stillness. Because they live high in the sacred mountains, they are known for attracting other sacred spirits and will teach their witch the art of calling and working with these entities.

The jaguar is the gatekeeper to the unknown and the mystical, and is a force of raw, primal energy. As an animal guide, they can show you how to access the Akashic records and even walk into your past lives. The Akashic records are a compilation of everything that has ever happened throughout the Universe, including thoughts, words, and emotions of every entity and life-form, not just humans, for the past, present, and future. Jaguars will teach their charge how to reclaim their power by awakening that inner core energy. They are the embodiment of both the Moon and the Sun and, through that, are able to teach balance and show how to walk between and within liminal spaces.

Intense energy surrounds the jaguar and makes for a particularly powerful familiar. They are known for ruling the Underworld—considered the land without light in some cultures—and because of this, they gift their witch with the ability to pierce the veil of darkness and reach into it for power. This is not black magick but akin to calling upon dark goddess energies. Because they are the mystical gatekeepers, they take on the role of showing the witch their path and purpose and guiding them along it. They embody lunar energy and aid in Moon magick as well as boost psychic abilities, intuition, and the ability to face the darkness head-on.

The cheetah is the fastest land mammal, reaching speeds of 75 miles per hour (121 km/h), and can also outpace most race cars with an acceleration speed of 0 to 64 miles per hour (103 km/h) in just three seconds. This energy is all about fast action and quick decisions. It is also a reminder that we must pace ourselves.

With the cheetah by your side as a guide, they will teach you not only the art of trusting your instincts when it comes to quick decision making, but also how vital it can be to act quickly in certain situations. A cheetah's spine is the most flexible of the cats and gives them a biological advantage to increase their speed. This adaptation teaches us the importance of remaining flexible in our own lives, giving us an advantage over rigid thinking and closed-mindedness.

As a familiar, the cheetah will help their witch learn how to properly use their own energy and magick. They will remind you that sometimes swift and easy is better than something long and drawn out. The witch will learn snap-fast spells for protecting themselves, their energy, and their home with a cheetah familiar. They will lend bursts of lightning-speed energy, confidence in your own abilities, and show you how to react or adapt to situations where quick magick would be the most useful.

The tiger is the largest of the big cats. A tiger's energy is a powerful force of strength, control, and determination. Like the leopard and jaguar whose spots are like fingerprints of individuality, so too are the tiger's stripes. Because tigers love water, they also emanate this fluid energy, bringing in strong emotional support.

The stripes of a tiger are not symmetrical nor do they follow any sort of pattern. The stripes on the left do not mirror those on the right. Because of this, a tiger animal guide will teach you that you are beautiful just the way you are and to embrace your uniqueness. The tiger helps guide you to emotional stability and through their gentle chuffles, a contentment sound unique to big cats, especially tigers, and enables their charge to effectively communicate these emotions to others. Because they have large territories that they must protect, tigers teach us what it means to be able to set and maintain healthy boundaries.

If you have this powerful cat as a familiar, you could very well be blessed with "second sight." Tigers have "false eyes" on the back of their ears, thus giving the illusion that they can see in all directions. Because of their large size, tigers cannot chase their prey for very long. Instead, they rely on strategy and patience, and will bring this energy to their witch. They offer the wisdom of knowing when to act and how. They teach us about divine and universal timing and that things come to us when they are meant to. Like a tiger guide, a tiger familiar will help the witch maintain boundaries. They will bestow their magick upon the witch to create powerful wards and shields.

Mountain lion, cougar, puma. As their name suggests, the mountain lion makes their home in rocky, craggy, mountainous areas. Because of this, they are known to be one with Mother Earth and act as guardians of the mountains. They can scale steep rock faces quickly, bringing an energy of balance and agility. Mountain lions roam from Canada to Argentina, fostering adaptability and self-reliance. As messengers, they come to us when we need to be shown how to find our balance. They also appear to tell us that we should not be afraid of reaching for something higher, something that will take us to the next level and bring us into our power.

When we are blessed with mountain lion as our animal guide, we will get reminders of "look before you leap," to take a breath and come back to center before making a next move. Because the mountain lion is the big cat that can purr, they teach us the meaning of contentment and how to find enjoyment and satisfaction in life. They also show us how to be fierce when needed.

Working with a mountain lion as a familiar helps witches focus their intentions and strength, using their power wisely. The mountain lion gifts their witch with bold earth energy and shows them how to interact with it and use it in spell work. The witch is likely to take up the mantle as an Earth guardian as well and will be able to call upon the strength and power of the mountains. A mountain lion familiar will help the witch stay grounded while being able to bring forth large amounts of energy.

Other big cats not previously mentioned are the bobcat, lynx, serval, clouded leopard, caracal, and ocelot. There are other smaller wild cats too. All the cats have varying energies and can share different aspects of magick with you. It is important to remember that each one is to be respected, regardless of their size.

WORKING WITH BIG CAT ENERGY

When we work with big cat energy, the experience will be profound and magickal. These powerful creatures have been coming to the aid of witches, shamans, and other magickal people for millennia. There are stories that have been relayed of shocking interactions with big cats in the wild, within wildlife sanctuaries, and even at zoos. Looking directly into the eyes of a mountain lion as she delivers her message is something that stays with you long after the experience has ended.

As witches, we have the ability to call this energy to us. We can invoke the power of the lion when we need courage. We can call upon the black panther when we need to work within the shadows and darkness. We may work with just the energy of the animal or call the spirit of that animal to us. We can invite them into our magick circle to aid us in spell work or ask them to walk with us when we need that extra guidance and support.

You can refer to the list that is provided beginning on page 69 regarding the various energies and aspects of the big cats. There is also a lot of information available online about each individual cat as an animal messenger or guide. If you are unsure as to which one you should call upon, use the simple spell on page 68 to invoke the big cat that you need at the moment. Have faith that the one that shows up is what you require, and remember that the most important thing is to be open to their messages and teachings.

Again, if you are unsure whether a big cat is your familiar, you can use the simple spell on page 68 to reveal your familiar to you.

Whether they come as a messenger, guide, or familiar, big cats are to be treasured and revered. Remember that we do not choose them, they choose us.

If you know which cat needs to be called, the following poems for the individual big cats will serve as their invocation, calling their energies and spirit to you. There are also recommended candle colors to burn while calling in each energy. The candle colors noted either align directly with the energy of the big cat or the colors of that specific big cat. **Note:** These are not spells but invocations and can be used at any time, with or without the candle, to call the specific big cat energy to you in a time of need. Remember that invocations only call the energy to you while a spell is incorporating that energy into a working using magick. If you would like to use candles with your work, see page 142 for a reference on candle color meanings to best match your intention with your spell work.

Ritual to Invoke Big Cat Energy

Use this general ritual to invoke the big cat energy that is required in that moment.

YOU WILL NEED

- Pen
- Notebook or journal

DIRECTIONS

1. Go within your sacred space.
2. Cast a circle.
3. Intone the following chant three times:

> *Fierce and bold*
> *With beauty untold*
> *Your strength this circle will hold*
> *Powerful and mighty*
> *Big cat energy*
> *I ask that you come to me.*
> *As I will, so mote it be (after the third time).*

4. Be aware of who shows up for you. Write down any messages or impressions. Let them know why you have called them and remember to ask for their permission if you would like to use their energy in spell work. If they consent, then proceed with the working.
5. Thank the cat that showed up for their assistance and bid them farewell.
6. Open the circle.

TIP Appropriate offerings include small amounts of raw meat (given outside), Moon water (water left under the moonlight during your chosen Moon phase, usually the Full Moon, to infuse it with Moon energy), Sun water for lion (water left in the sunlight for a certain period of time so that it is infused with Sun energy; make sure this water isn't too hot before using it for your workings), and catnip. Yes, big cats love catnip too.

Lion

Reciting this will invoke the power and energies of the lion.
Burn a yellow or gold candle.
Energies: Divine Masculine energies, Sun magick, protection

Do not be fooled
By his napping in the Sun
Beneath the golden coat
And mane untamed
A fierce protector
Lies in wait
Strength and courage unrivaled
Guardian of the pride
Walking in confidence
Hearing the lion's roar
Come what may.

Black Panther

Reciting this will invoke the power and energies of the black panther.
Burn a black candle.
Energies: Self-reliance, Moon magick, Divine Feminine energies

She moves silently through the night
Unseen, cloaked in darkness
Stalking the jungle with stealth
Presence revealed only when the time is right
Black panther, sacred Divine Feminine
And a force to be reckoned with.

Jaguar

Reciting this will invoke the power and energies of the jaguar.
Burn one black and one gold candle.
Energies: Awakening/reclaiming inner power, guidance, intuition

Fierce hunter of the night
With strength and grace she strikes
Jaguar, gatekeeper to the unknown
Mystic realms and awakening the soul
She sees beyond the veil
And shows one to their true self.

Leopard

Reciting this will invoke the power and energies of the leopard.
Burn one black candle and one tan or light brown candle.
Energies: Confidence, divination, intuition

She wears her spots with pride
From her true self she never hides
Fierce power, free and untamed
Leopard huntress stalks the night
On the ground or from a tree
Changing perception to truly see
With patience she waits
Hidden in plain sight.

Mountain Lion

Reciting this will invoke the power and energies of the mountain lion. Burn one tan or light brown candle.

Energies: Balance, adaptability, independence

Perched upon the craggy ledge
Her watchful golden eyes
Patience in the sacred hours
Dawn and dusk
The huntress awaits
Primal and feminine
Power and grace
Sensual and fierce
A perfect balance
Of body, mind, and spirit
Cougar stakes her claim.

Tiger

Reciting this will invoke the power and energies of the tiger.
Burn one orange candle and one black candle.
Energies: Strength, emotional stability, individuality

Fiery strength of will
Wild warrior of the jungle
Do not wake the sleeping tiger
Light and Dark
Balance of shadows
Power and grace.

Snow Leopard

Reciting this will invoke the power and energies of the snow leopard.
Burn a white or gray candle.
Energies: Wisdom, knowledge, sharp perception

Winds swirl
High in the Sacred Mountains
Where survival is the key
Resilient and elusive
Snow leopard, keeper of Ancient Wisdom
Guide to the sacred spirits.

Cheetah

Reciting this will invoke the power and energies of the cheetah.
Burn one yellow candle and one black candle.
Energies: Inner trust, quick action, flexibility

Chasing dreams at the speed of light
It's time to move, go now
Across the savannah
The cheetah's powerful stride
Never missing an opportunity
Trusting in her decisions.

A Being of the Metaphysical

The energy of the cat is not really something that can simply be put into words. They are the "other," the magickal and mysterious. They belong to the metaphysical and astral realms and even realms that we humans have not yet ventured into.

There is a good reason why witches and other magickal people love to work with felines. As we have already learned, cats have a long and illustrious history tied to the occult and the world of the metaphysical. Many believe that felines are more attuned to energies, entities, and auras than any other animal. Thousands of people across the globe have witnessed their cat get up randomly and stare at nothing. Why is this? Simply put, they are beings that can peer beyond the veil and into other realms.

While other animals have the ability to see and feel energies, they do not compare to the cat. It is true that both dogs and cats have heightened senses regarding sight, hearing, and smell, but it is the long whiskers of the feline that give them a physiological advantage. Their whiskers are highly sensitive and pick up energetic changes or varying vibrational patterns. It is believed that the overall energy and vibration of felines themselves add to their enhanced ability to see into the "other." Witches, shamans, and magickal people know that vibration is everything. Crystals, plants, and animals all have different frequencies. It makes sense that an animal with an innate ability to pick up on subtle vibrations, energies, auras, and such would have a frequency that is more attuned to those of the metaphysical realm.

Pay close attention to how cats are behaving, especially in a home or personal space. When a cat is seemingly staring intently at nothing, this typically means that there is an energy or entity present there. It has been reported that the cat will sense the entity and then the person will feel the cool spot, a light will flicker, or an item will move. If the cat suddenly hisses or lets out a low yowl or growling sound, beware! They have picked up on an energy that is negative, potentially aggressive, or just plain unfriendly and they are warning you and the entity to stay back.

Portals are another hot topic when it comes to our feline friends. Portals are gateways that lead to other realms, realities, or dimensions. These can be opened unknowingly or on purpose. Cats are extremely sensitive when it comes to portals and their energies. Cats, especially those that are familiars, have been known to stand guard to ensure that nothing passes through that means us harm. If you ever notice your feline friend returning to the same location in the home repeatedly to just sit, usually looking at a wall or the ceiling, this could mean that there is a portal there. Ask your cat to help you close it and then burn an herb that helps cleanse the space, such as common garden sage, rosemary, or pine. Please call for backup if you feel this portal is beyond your expertise. As a side note, spirit boards or Ouija boards are known for opening portals. Individuals have witnessed cats becoming quite agitated when a spirit board is being used. People have reported cats sitting on the board, knocking off the planchette, knocking the board over altogether, and even growling or hissing at it. If a cat is acting out of sorts while a spirit board is in use, discontinue the session and immediately cleanse the area.

Cats not only act as guardians and furry alarm systems for spirit activity, but they also help cleanse the space and their human. The frequency or vibration of cats is one that naturally repels and transmutes negative energies. You might notice your cat will patrol the home, going from room to room. This is their way of reading the energies and dispelling any heavy or negative vibes from the home or space. A cat's purr is also an effective tool when it comes to cleansing an area. If the feline senses you are in need,

they will sit on you and purr. The vibration caused by the purr immediately breaks up any heaviness in your energetic field. If the cat rubs their body against objects that you have just brought home, such as your purse or briefcase, they are likely trying to cleanse the object of energies that have been picked up throughout the day before it can contaminate the area. When they rub against your leg, they are sharing their aura and absorbing negative energies from you.

While it may not be a frequent concern, the presence of a cat in the home can protect the residents from any hexes or curses that might be placed upon them. They can also stop psychic attacks meant to cause harm to their humans. The cat's powerful auric field will absorb any negative energies that are being sent and transmute them. Between clearing negative vibes in the home, stopping curses in their tracks, and helping with aura cleansing, a cat expends a significant amount of their own energy. This is the reason for the catnap. They use this time to transmute the energies they have absorbed and then recharge their batteries. Help your cat out by regularly cleansing the home or space as well as your own energy.

Many people say that cats are more discerning than dogs when it comes to giving their affection. Cats often act aloof or refuse to interact altogether. This could be because cats can see and sense auras. They may choose to not interact closely when the aura is mucky. The exception to this is with their chosen human(s). They will watch the auras or energy fields of those within the home. If their human's aura has been affected negatively, they will often come to them seemingly seeking attention, but in reality they are trying to help them cleanse heavy energies. They may curl up in your lap or sit on your chest to clear the aura, often purring. When they sense or see something in the aura of an unknown person that poses an energetic threat to them, they will typically hide. If the cat hisses at someone, take note. They are aware that something is going on with this person that makes them uncomfortable. This is a warning and likely an energy that you are not sensing yourself. Never make your cat interact with anyone if they choose not to; there is a reason why they are leery of them.

Because a cat's energy, aura, and overall vibration align with the metaphysical world, it is no wonder that they are naturally drawn to spiritual people. Witches, shamans, and other magickal humans also have a frequency that opens them up to higher energies and realms. Have you ever gone to someone's home and their cat takes an immediate liking to you? Their person might tell you that they never like strangers, but here they are, rubbing against your leg or curled in your lap. They like your vibe. Those that work magick and/or have spiritual practices tend to keep their energetic field "neater and cleaner" than those who do not. This is one of the reasons why cats are drawn to them. With spiritual people, cats simply have an easier time because they are not having to constantly clear the energetic field or raise their vibration. They can simply be, and that is a beautiful thing to them. It is believed that cats "know" they too are magickal beings and they want to share this magick with us.

With their link to higher energies and realms, cats are the only animals, other than familiars, that will not disturb a magickal cast circle. They are naturally drawn to this energy and will be curious about what is going on. They can come and go as they please through the circle without any interruption in the energy field. This is because cats can raise their own vibration to "match the magick." Even if higher magick is being worked along with complex spells or rituals, the cat will match it, power for power. You can test this yourself. Cast a circle and be very cognizant of where the boundaries are. Begin a simple magickal working and see how long it takes your cat to wander in. Watch as they cross back and forth over the circle's boundaries without any disruption in energy. However, magick can be like catnip for them, so be prepared for a giddy kitten. If you have another pet, such as a dog, you can test the difference. Note how it feels when they cross the line of the circle. Without a door being cut, you will feel the energetic shift as the dog moves about, into or out of the circle.

As we have previously learned, the association between witches and cats goes back centuries. While most of the previous ties have a negative connotation, today's relationship between witches and cats is centered around common mystical, metaphysical, and magickal ideals. With two beings having vibrations that align with the higher realms, it is no wonder that they seek out one another. Because of these mutual links to patterns of higher vibrations, the energy exchange between cats and witches is one of ease, both give and take. Their relationship is highly symbiotic.

Remember that both cats and witches are associated with the night, a time shrouded in mystery and magick. The "witching hour" is between midnight and three in the morning. While some rituals are done during this time, most witches are getting their zzzzs. The witch's cat, however, is up and on the prowl. The nocturnal nature of the feline naturally aligns them with the Moon. Moon energy is feminine and corresponds to the Divine Feminine. Many witches work with Moon and goddess energy, so having a cat as a friend or familiar can strengthen the relationship with lunar energy and, through that, the divine feminine. A witch's cat can also aid in lunar workings and magicks. Moon energy can be associated with emotions, intuition, dreams, visions, illuminating what needs to be seen, releasing and cleansing, and, of course, the Divine Feminine.

Ritual to Sync with Lunar Energies

Here is a simple spell to help you sync with the energy of the Moon and the lunar vibration of your feline familiar. This spell should be worked at night. If possible, be in an area where you can see the Moon.

YOU WILL NEED

- A small silver candle
- Lighter or matches
- Your cat

DIRECTIONS

1. Go into your sacred space.
2. Place the silver candle on your altar.
3. Cast a circle.
4. Bring the image of a full, glowing Moon into your mind. Visualize the moonbeams shining down.
5. Light the silver candle and intone the following:

> *Goddess of the Moon*
> *Feline bathed in silver light*
> *With your energy I attune*
> *Give to me the sight*
> *Intuition, visions, and dreams*
> *Together we stalk the night*
> *Through her magickal beams.*

6. Hold your cat for as long as they will allow you to and focus on the silver candle.
7. Let the candle burn out.
8. Thank the Moon, goddess, Divine Feminine, and your cat for being there and for their assistance.
9. Open the circle.

While the vibrational pattern of felines is typically feminine in nature, remember that there is one exception—the lion. As we have learned, the lion aligns with the energy of the Sun and holds masculine energy. This brings balance—yin and yang. Sun and lion energy confer joy, creativity, courage, vitality, and the Divine Masculine. Your cat can also tap into this leonine energy and facilitate synchronization for you.

Ritual to Sync with Solar Energies

The following spell will help you align with the energy of the Sun and the lion. This spell should be worked during the day. If possible, be in an area where the Sun is shining brightly into the room.

YOU WILL NEED

- A small gold candle
- Your cat
- Lighter or matches

DIRECTIONS

1. Go into your sacred space.
2. Place the gold candle on your altar.
3. Cast a circle.
4. Bring the image of a warm summer day into your mind. Visualize the Sun shining brightly and feel his warmth upon your skin.
5. Ask your cat to help you harness the energy of the lion and the Sun; notice the characteristics that are the same between the cat and a lion. Do not be alarmed if the cat morphs into an image of a lion at this point. They are doing what you have asked and are bringing in that leonine vibration.

6. Light the gold candle and intone the following:

Rays of the Sun, bright and hot
Shining upon his golden mane
Passion and courage, fear is naught
Creative and vital, not to tame
Happiness and joy he brings
Sun god energy aflame
A mighty roar from lion rings.

7. Bring your hands up near the candle on either side of it so you can feel its warmth but not get burned.
8. Continue to gaze upon the gold candle and its flame.
9. Once you feel the Sun/lion energy present, drop your hands and let the candle burn out.
10. Thank the Sun, god, Divine Masculine, lion, and your cat for being there and for their assistance.
11. Open the circle.

If you have already performed either of the two spells on page 83 or above, you may have felt your cat acting as an energetic conduit. For such a small animal, they are a powerhouse when it comes to being able to run energy through their bodies. When they are in circle with you, they can and will serve as a battery, so to speak, for your magickal workings. Because their energy aligns with that of the higher realms, they can easily access it and funnel it to the practitioner or into the working itself. If the cat is your familiar, they will give this willingly and without you needing to ask permission. If the feline is simply your companion, you can still work with them in this manner; however, you should ask their permission before proceeding. If they choose to allow it, they will stay in the space with you while you work. If not, they will leave.

As previously mentioned, cats will often guard open portals. They are fiercely protective of their humans and their space when it comes to negative energies and entities. They will also serve as a protector while a witch is in circle. You may not be actively working with your feline at the time, but they may choose to stay near to monitor energy levels. Because they can readily see the witch's aura and surrounding energy, they can help disperse anything that could potentially harm or overwhelm the practitioner. If you notice the cat walking widdershins (counterclockwise) in the area where you are working magick, know that they are working to break up the energies there. You may need to proceed with caution if the cat becomes agitated during this time. This could be a warning that things are not quite right.

Cats, while nocturnal by nature, will often nap with or near you while you are sleeping. We are most vulnerable during our nonwaking hours, and cats are aware of this. They choose to be near us during that time to offer protection. Some people are prone to astral travel while asleep. The cat is there to guard your physical being and the tether to your spirit that is otherwise occupied in the astral realm. Felines also serve as an anchor to this world while you travel. This also holds true if you are engaged in shamanic journey work. You can ask your cat to act as your timer to bring you back or they can gently call you out of the journey if they feel that you have been gone too long. A cat can also sense when their human is having a bad dream. People have reported that suddenly their cat will show up in their dream and then they wake up. The cat is traveling into the dream/astral world to assist and guide you back.

All of the metaphysical, mystical, magickal properties of the feline makes them one of the most powerful familiars you could have. It is also because of these properties that familiar spirits choose to take on the form of a cat. Remember that familiar spirits choose to work with you and not every cat that chooses a witch is a familiar. Having a cat that is also your familiar is a beautiful thing. There is such a deep connection and bond there. A lot of witches will tell you that they can communicate with their feline familiar telepathically. The cat will send simple words or images to their person and vice versa. Being able to communicate in this way strengthens the bond. It is also especially helpful when the cat needs to let their person know quickly that something is wrong.

While all cats are magickal and can lend their support, the magickal energy summoned when working with a feline familiar is unsurpassed. Learning how to work with them can bring things to your practice that you may not have known were possible. Let them teach you; let them guide you. Open yourself to their magick and, in turn, they will open themselves to yours.

Your Feline Familiar and You

When you are blessed with a familiar, it is a true gift from the Universe. To have a familiar spirit choose to reincarnate to continue their work with you is something miraculous.

If you have found that you do indeed have a feline familiar, then you are one of the truly blessed. This is not to take away from familiars that come in other forms, only to say that the bond with a cat familiar and the magick that can be worked with them at your side is something to be marveled at because, again, they choose us, we do not choose them.

Just because you are now aware that a familiar spirit has chosen you doesn't mean that they have come into your life yet. If you are still waiting for your cat familiar, remember that everything comes in the time that it is meant to. However, there is a simple spell that you can perform to call your familiar to you.

Ritual to Call Your Feline Familiar to You

Use this ritual to call your familiar to you. Be advised that this working must come after you have performed the Ritual to Reveal Your Feline Familiar to You (see page 48) for it to be of benefit to you.

YOU WILL NEED

- Cat candle or generic cat figurine/photo
- Lighter or matches (if needed)
- A timer (it is acceptable to set a timer on your phone)

TIP Once again, if you can find a cat candle, it is recommended for this working. If not, a generic cat figurine or photo will work as well. It is important not to have anything too distinct because you may not know exactly what the cat looks like yet. Think silhouettes of cats instead of a photo of a tabby.

DIRECTIONS

1. Go into your sacred space.
2. Place the candle or cat figurine/photo on your altar.
3. Cast a circle.
4. Focus on the energy you felt when you performed the Ritual to Reveal Your Feline Familiar to You (page 48).
5. Light the candle if using it or hold the figurine/photo and intone the following three times:

> *To my familiar I wish to bond*
> *I call you from the beyond*
> *Being of Spirit and being of power*
> *Come to me in the right and ready hour*
> *The feline form you take*
> *Bringing magick in your wake.*
> *As I will, so mote it be (after the third time).*

6. Set the timer for nine minutes and let the candle burn, then snuff it out (or continue to hold the figurine/ photo for that amount of time).
7. Open the circle.

Pay attention now that you have called your feline familiar to you. If you have the sudden urge to visit a pet adoption, then go. See a sign for free kittens? Call to set up a time to meet them. Don't overthink it; just be open and feel. This is the Universe's way of helping you, as well as the familiar spirit trying to make their way to you.

BEING OPEN TO MESSAGES

Remember that your feline familiar will also act as a messenger and a guide for you. If you perform the spell to call them to you, and you are now suddenly dreaming of a cat in a specific location, this is more than likely your familiar communicating with you. They are sending the message of how to find them.

Once you have finally found your way to one another, you can immediately start bonding with your familiar. One way is by talking with them. Remember that this lets them know that you are open to communicating with them. Don't be surprised if you pick up your little ball of fur only to get an image of a can of tuna. They are testing how best to communicate with you and deliver messages. Sometimes it will be through images and sometimes it may come as words in your mind. They might also lead you directly to something. For instance, you cannot find the incense you want to use for a ritual and you find yourself asking out loud where it could be. Your cat suddenly jumps up onto the bookcase and is pawing at the back edge. When you pull the bookcase out slightly, you realize that the incense box fell behind there. Voilà! Your familiar has led you directly to what you need.

Once you have created this bond with your feline familiar, you will notice that you suddenly seem more plugged into the world of Spirit than ever. Messages come through more clearly and more frequently. Your dreams may be more vivid and you may recall them easier. This is what it means to have a cat familiar: they are facilitating communication between the higher realms of Spirit and you. They act as the go-between. Remember that cats are naturally attuned to these energies and when your familiar comes in feline form, this attunement is even greater.

How can you learn to listen to these messages? Simply put, be open. Don't discount the things that are coming through. Society conditions us that it is "crazy" to listen to voices that come through and even crazier to trust and follow them. Your feline familiar has chosen you and that is a beautiful thing. Let them do what they came into physical form to do, and part of that is to deliver these messages to you.

To start out, keep a journal of messages, impressions, images, etc. Note the date and time and whether there is any later outcome to each one. For example, you kiss your kitten goodbye and suddenly know that you should not take a certain road to work that day. You follow this message and take a different route to work. You later learn that there was an accident that happened just as you would have been passing through. This message could have been a simple warning about traffic that would have made you late, or something greater that saved you from being in the wrong place at the wrong time and getting into said accident. The more you document, the more you will figure out what messages are coming through from your familiar and how they are relating to your life. For some, this is a vital step because it is confirmation that what is happening isn't something that is just in their head.

Messages that your feline is delivering aren't always warnings. Sometimes it has to do with a spell or ritual timing. There could be messages that are from an ancestor or another guide that you have yet to make contact with. Your cat familiar may also deliver messages from other entities, such as the fae, land wights (land spirits), or elementals (spirits or entities of earth, water, fire, or air). They can also deliver messages from departed loved ones.

Remember that your feline familiar is also here to serve as your guide. Notice the messages that are guiding you, such as a spell or a particular herb to use. They will also guide you on your path. If you meet an individual that seems like a spiritual person but your cat does not like them, that is probably a sign that they are not part of your path. Every spell we work, every ritual we perform, and all the intentions that we are setting are part of our path. If you are getting messages about how to go about these, take note because this is your familiar helping you align with that path and your purpose here.

If you are having issues hearing the messages or are finding it difficult to receive them in general, try this simple ritual to facilitate openness.

Ritual to Open Crown Chakra

Use this ritual to open up your crown chakra to help you receive messages.

YOU WILL NEED

- A purple candle (the color purple aligns with the crown chakra)
- A carrier oil of your choice to dress the candle
- Dried mugwort
- Dried clary sage
- Lighter or matches
- A timer (it is acceptable to set a timer on your phone)
- Pen and notebook or journal

DIRECTIONS

1. Go into your sacred space.
2. Rub the candle with the carrier oil and then roll it in the dried herbs.
3. Place the candle on your altar.
4. Cast a circle.
5. Light the candle and intone the following three times:

> *Messages coming to me*
> *Help me so that I can see*
> *Delivered by feline familiar*
> *Help me so that I can hear*
> *From the Divine, Universe, and Spirit*
> *Help me so that I am open to it.*
> *As I will, so mote it be (after the third time).*

6. Set a timer for nine minutes.
7. Soften your gaze if you feel comfortable, or close your eyes, and clear your mind.
8. When the timer is done, write down any messages that may have come through in your notebook or journal.
9. Let the candle burn out completely.
10. Open the circle.

TEACHERS

There are so many lessons that our furry feline friends bring to us throughout the time that is shared. Some of these lessons are more mundane, but nonetheless important.

Our feline familiars teach us about boundaries, how to set them and how to maintain them. If a cat does not want to be touched, they will let you know. If you continue to try to push their boundaries, they will attack. They teach us that independence is important but that it is also okay to be taken care of and to receive love. Your cat will show you that there is a time for play, a time to hunt, and a need to rest and that a catnap is never a bad thing!

Our familiars teach us to believe in ourselves, our power, our intuition, and our ability to send and receive messages. They are teaching us to believe in the magick that is all around us and the magick that lives within us. They show us that the magick is always there, and they teach us how to access it. They will teach us how to reach into the void and manifest our desires and the life we want. This is alchemy at its finest and they are gifting it to us.

THE SUPPORT OF A MAGICKAL BEING

It's hard to imagine that an eight-pound ball of fur will be one of our greatest allies and biggest supporters in the magickal world. A familiar chooses a witch and comes into their physical form with the agreement that they are here to teach and guide, deliver messages, assist, protect, and lend power and magick to workings. Remember that while they most often appear to be a sweet and cuddly little creature, the feline that has adopted you actually houses an incredibly powerful spiritual entity.

As mentioned in the previous chapter, a familiar can and will act as an energetic conduit for their witch. This is especially evident when magickal workings are being done. Once you and your familiar are bonded, you should be able to tell when the familiar is pouring their magick or energy into a spell.

Because of the intense energy and higher levels of magick that are able to be worked alongside a feline familiar, it is advised to always cast a circle for these workings. Remember that a cat moving in and out of the circle does not disturb it. Some cats may choose to sit front and center within the circle while others hang back, appearing to be just a simple spectator. Make no mistake, if they are in the room with you, they are interested in the magick. If the feline is in the room when the circle is being cast, you might feel them adding to the boundaries and protection of the circle. There are times when the physical cat may not want to participate in the spell or ritual, but you can still call the energy of the familiar spirit into the circle. Have no fear, this will not bring any harm to the cat in any way.

Ritual to Call Your Familiar's Energy into the Circle

Use this ritual to call your familiar's energy into the circle to assist with and enhance your spell work. This spell may change your cat's mind about their participation but does not affect their free will. Remember that the familiar spirit resides within the cat and the energy of the familiar spirit can be called separately without any harm to the cat that serves as their vessel. It also works for familiars that do not exist in a physical form.

DIRECTIONS

1. Go into your sacred space.
2. Cast a circle.
3. Intone the following:

> *The circle has been cast*
> *I call upon your power vast*
> *Within the boundaries I have set*
> *Working with no threat*
> *Magickal familiar of mine*
> *I ask that you join me at this time*
> *As I will, so mote it be.*

4. Complete whatever the spell working is.
5. Thank your familiar for their assistance.
6. Open the circle.

TIP ⟨ Cat treats, catnip, and, of course, tuna or salmon are always wonderful offerings for a hardworking feline familiar.

MAGICKAL BUFFER AND GUARDIAN

The more that you work with your familiar, the more comfortable it will feel and you will begin to notice more of the things they do without being asked. One of the benefits of a cat familiar is that they act as a buffer for the magick that is taking place. Even with a protective circle in place, you usually need to clear and cleanse a magickal space after a working. With a feline familiar, you will find that the need to clear and cleanse becomes less and less necessary. They automatically keep the energy flowing throughout a ritual or spell and then help clear it out afterward, ensuring that any residue is taken care of. Over time, you might also find that the need to use cleansing herb smoke throughout the house declines as well. A feline familiar will also help you (their witch) keep your (their) energetic field clear. This doesn't mean that you should forgo energetic cleansing altogether and the feline familiar will appreciate it not being solely delegated to them.

Cats take protecting their territory seriously, so they do a wonderful job of keeping dark entities or negative spirits away from the home. The auric field of a cat is naturally repelling toward unsavory spiritual guests. If something does make its way in, your familiar will let you know and then help you deal with it. They will guide you as to how to go about it and then lend you the power and magick required. They will also make you aware of any portals or vortices that need attention, will help redirect any energies that are coming through, and then help close it.

Because your feline familiar is a fierce protector, you can ask for assistance when it comes to securing the wards (magickal defense system) around the home. Your feline familiar will provide power and magick to reinforce what is already in place and also show how it can be even stronger. Notice that your feline will often do "laps" around the home. This is how they check the wards. They will infuse it with power and magick as they see fit if it needs any adjustments. If you have a crystal grid set up for home protection, the familiar can also help seal it with their own protection magick.

⸻ PSYCHIC BOND ⸻

Checking in frequently with your feline familiar in regard to the energy of the home and about magickal things in general will help you further strengthen the bond between you. Remember, it is through this bond that they are connecting with you and delivering messages as well as lending power and magick. The stronger the bond, the more easily and effectively the two of you will be able to communicate.

This bond, between familiar and witch, when it is particularly strong creates a psychic link that can be stretched for miles. The benefit of this is that you can both send and receive messages at a distance, and your familiar can lend power and guidance if you need it.

There are stories of this psychic link warning the witch or even giving aid from a long distance. A friend of mine shared a story of a witch they knew hearing their cat hiss (their cat was at home) as they were walking to their car at night, the hair rising on their neck, and then having the knowledge that someone or something was just warned to get away. This link is important and can be strengthened over time and by working with your familiar. With each message they deliver that you successfully interpret, each spell worked together, and even the evening cuddles, your bond grows and becomes more powerful. To help facilitate and bolster this link, use the following ritual.

Ritual to Strengthen the Bond with Your Familiar

Use this ritual to strengthen the bond between yourself and your familiar.

YOU WILL NEED

- A purple candle
- Lighter or matches
- Your feline familiar in the room with you

DIRECTIONS

1. Go into your sacred space.
2. Place the candle on your altar.
3. Cast a circle.
4. Light the candle.
5. Hold your cat close if they will let you and intone the following three times:

> *The link between familiar and witch*
> *Closer and stronger we do stitch*
> *Messages and images we need to share*
> *We seek now to be more aware*
> *Through our beings it will lace*
> *As the psychic bond snaps in place.*
> *As I will, so mote it be (after the third time).*

6. Let the candle burn out.
7. Open the circle.

MY PERSONAL EXPERIENCE
⟶ WITH MY FAMILIAR ⟶

As I mentioned in the introduction, my familiar is in their fourth incarnation with me. When my beloved dog passed over the Rainbow Bridge in the summer of 2017, I was devastated. She was my familiar then too. Later, at Samhain, her spirit came to me and told me that she would come back to me. She showed me her previous incarnations, one of them being a feisty little cat named Little Bit, and all that she'd been to me throughout those lifetimes with the promise of her return. I had a feeling she would come back to me as a cat.

I looked on pet adoption websites and went to two different adoptions at the local pet stores and still couldn't find her. It wasn't until October 2021 when I went to Texas (from Colorado) to visit friends that I would find my familiar again. My friends were hosting pet adoptions at their brewery during a street festival, and I was helping them set up the tents and get the animals settled. I opened up the back of the pet cargo van and saw her precious little face and said, "Oh! There you are!" She reached for me with her tiny little paw through the bars and it was instant love. At the time, I wondered how I would get her back to Colorado. As it turned out, the adoption worker told me that they were in Denver once a month and would be happy to deliver her to me. This witch was reunited with her familiar on Samhain, 2021.

I named my familiar cat Artemis after the Greek goddess of the hunt and she doesn't let me forget that she is to be worshipped. I have felt her power as a familiar spirit since the very first day. From the time she was a kitten, her magick has amazed me. She protects me when I sleep, often lying on me physically to keep me anchored from astral traveling.

I have felt her energy surround me when I was rushed by three different spirits needing to be crossed over even though we were not in each other's presence at that moment. Artemis sits with me for every ritual and every spell, lending energy and just enjoying the magick that is in the air. She communes with my animal guides and has even delivered messages from Spirit. She regularly checks the wards on our home to ensure we're safe from any magickal or spiritual attacks. She sends me images to communicate but can also put the words right into my mind. There is no doubt of her magickal abilities. The adorable little fur ball that houses a powerful supernatural being completely has my heart.

The Power of a Cat's Magick

Every cat is magickal, not just those that house a familiar spirit. They are disguised as little balls of fur, but in reality, they have some pretty spectacular superpowers.

E ven as kittens, these magnificent creatures hold a tremendous amount of power. If you have been working the included spells, you are beginning to sense that, if you didn't already know it. While the energy and bond of a feline companion are different than that of an animal guide and familiar, remember that your "muggle" cat is no muggle at all. They still hold their own magick. This magick can be found in every part of them, including shed items, such as fur, claws, and whiskers.

If you are lucky enough to find shed items from your cat, be sure to keep them, as they hold powerful magick. And yes, there is something that all that shed fur can be used for as well. While cat nail clippings can also be used, DO NOT EVER cut or pluck a cat's whiskers!

CAT FUR COLORS

As witches, we know that everything is energy and those energies are different and varied depending on the object. Clear quartz feels different and holds different energies than rose quartz does, yet they are both types of quartz crystals. As mentioned earlier, we use different candle colors in spell work because each color aligns with a different energy. The same can be true of cats. We have learned that the big cats all possess varying energies and vibrations. Domestic cats of different colors or breeds can have distinct vibrational patterns as well. The following is a breakdown of domestic cat colors and the energetic powers they possess.

Black Cats: The color black typically corresponds to protection, the night, the occult, and magick. Black cats excel at protection and keeping negative entities and energies away. These cats are known for being "witch cats." They are powerhouses when it comes to lending energy as a familiar. Because of their black fur, they are masters at blending into the shadows. Use their fur in spells for cloaking and shape-shifting.

Red/Orange/Yellow Cats: These colors represent vitality and correspond to Sun and Mars energy. Regardless of the sex of the feline, they might exude a more masculine energy because their coloring aligns with the Divine Masculine. Their shed fur can be used in Sun magick workings and spells for action, focus, and success.

 Blue Gray/Smoky Cats: Gray is a variance of silver and, as such, corresponds to the Divine Feminine and goddess energy. Because this color is a mixture, the cats hold the energy of balance. It is also a shadow color and represents the "in between." Use their fur in spell work for balance, shadow work, and traveling into the liminal spaces.

 White Cats: White is the color of healing and a feline of this color excels at it. It also represents purity. White aligns with lunar energies. White cats have long symbolized spiritual enlightenment or rebirth. Use white cat fur for healing spells or in charm or mojo bags for illness. Their fur can also be used for gaining access to your Akashic Records to promote spiritual and soul growth.

 Brown Cats: Solid brown cats are more rare than the other colorings. Brown represents Earth energy. Use brown cat fur in spells that require calming, grounding energy. It can also be kept in a locket or vial to help you feel calm and grounded.

Color Point (Siamese) Cats: These cats are considered "royal cats" by many. They represent luxury (wealth and prosperity), power, and wise leadership. Use their shed fur in money spells as well as to help guide you if you find yourself in a leadership role.

Persian Cats: Like Siamese cats, Persian cats represent wealth and prosperity. They also hold the energy of comfort, good luck, and good fortune. They have been known to be popular cats around business for this reason. Their fur can be used in money and good luck spells, as well as for good fortune in business.

 Calico (Tricolor) Cats: The traditional coloring of white, red, and black represents the three aspects of the goddess: the maiden (white), the mother (red for blood), and the crone (black for wisdom and magick). These cats hold the energy of all three colors. They are known to be powerful and highly intuitive. They make excellent messengers of the goddess. Use their fur when trying to connect to your own inner goddess or to balance the Divine Feminine within you.

 Two-Tone or Tuxedo Cats: This cat color is all about balance, as it holds both black and white cat energies. These cats also carry a little bit of mischief, urging us to keep the work/play balance in our lives. Use their fur for healing, spells for balance, and to help promote a positive, healthy mind-set around downtime and time for play.

Tortoiseshell Cats: Because this color pattern is (almost) only inherited by females, tortoiseshell cats are all about women's magick. They are the goddess, the Divine Feminine. They are highly clairvoyant and are protectors of children. Use their fur for strength and guidance to connect with the Divine Feminine within and your own feminine power as well as to connect with your general health as a woman. Their fur can help if you are in need of independence, especially in toxic relationships. It can also be used in healing work for feminine issues such as menstrual cycles. The fur is also extremely useful in protective charms for children.

 Tabby Cats: These cats tend to be social and adventurous. Indigenous Peoples believe that tabby cats are the keepers of the Universe's secrets and hold great wisdom. They also hold the energy of change and transformation. Use their fur for workings to help you "come out of your shell," for fortitude in social situations, or to have the courage to take needed risks. Use their shed fur for workings seeking wisdom and knowledge. If you are resisting change, use their fur to assist you with this so that the transition comes more easily.[11]

⚜══ Ritual to Create a Fur Talisman ══⚜

A talisman is an object imbued with magick through ritual or spell work that will grant protection from harm and can ward against negative or evil forces. It can also bring good luck.

To create a talisman, you must first decide what its purpose is. Once you know that, you can then collect or find the fur that you need. Don't be afraid to ask friends or family members for their cat's shed fur. If none of those cats' coloring corresponds to your need, then you might also be able to find it online. The next step is to figure out the container you would like to use for your talisman. Many people use lockets so that the talisman is worn without question in public settings. Small glass vials with stoppers are also a good choice.

YOU WILL NEED

- The container of your choice (locket or small glass vial with stopper)
- Incense
- Lighter or matches
- Shed cat fur in color that aligns with the talisman's purpose
- Candle, if using a glass vial, in the corresponding color to the spell work you are doing

DIRECTIONS

1. Cleanse the container of your choice with incense smoke by moving the vial through the smoke and then inserting the smoking end into the vial for a moment. Please use caution when using incense smoke.
2. Set the container and cat fur on your altar or in your sacred space.
3. Cast a circle.

4. Pick up the container and intone the following:

> *This [name the container—locket, vial, etc.] shall be for me*
> *A repository for this energy.*

5. Place the cat fur in the container as you intone the following:

> *The fur of the [name type of cat] I place in here*
> *To [name the working—heal, protect, bring good luck, etc.]*
> *A talisman I create*
> *Working for my aid.*
> *As I will, so mote it be.*

6. If you are using a glass vial, seal the stopper with candle wax. Using a corresponding color is recommended: black for protection, white for healing, etc. (See page 142 for more information on candle magick colors.) Open the circle.

TIP Use the talisman for its purpose, whether that means wearing it, placing it in the car, or gifting it to someone.

As a cat's claws grow, they shed the outer sheath. This is perfectly natural and means that their claws are healthy. You can collect the shed claw sheaths for magickal purposes. The first thing that may come to mind regarding a cat's claws is that they are for defense, and that would be accurate. Shed claws are perfect for protection spells. They can be added to spell jars, sachets, or even lockets that serve as an amulet or a talisman. You can even include shed claws in home protection mojo bags, grind them into a powder with other protective herbs, or just sprinkle them around the outside of the home.

If a witch needs to go on the offensive and fight, such as to break hexes and curses, claws are an excellent choice for this, as a cat will use them to attack if necessary. Include them in any working to effectively sever the bindings of a hex or curse. Cat claws used at the time of a Full or Waning Moon along with other cleansing herbs will add a powerful punch to spells or rituals for cutting away what is no longer serving you.

A feline also uses their claws to give them better traction, especially when they initially push off and as they gain momentum at higher speeds during a chase. Use shed claws in spell work to give you a jump start, help with traction, or gain momentum. Having trouble getting into your new workout plan? Maybe a little spell using shed claws will give you that "push off" you need along with helping to keep your stride once you get going.

Ritual to Create a Spell Jar for Protection

Use this spell jar to create a portable protection spell. This spell jar can be left on the altar or taken wherever it is needed, such as in the car or to work.

YOU WILL NEED

- Black candle
- Lighter or matches
- Pen and small piece of paper
- 2–3 shed cat claws
- Black obsidian
- Smoky quartz
- Dried sage
- Dried rosemary
- Cleansed small jar with lid or glass vial with stopper

DIRECTIONS

1. Go into your sacred space.
2. Cast a circle.
3. Light the black candle.
4. Write out exactly what the protection spell is for on the piece of paper.
5. Place the cat claws, crystals, and herbs into jar and chant the following:

> *From my guardian*
> *Claws to defend*
> *Protect and keep safe*
> *Herbs and stones lend their aid*
> *Wax to seal the spell in place*
> *[drizzle black candle wax to seal the stopper].*
> *So mote it be!*

6. Open the circle.

CAT TEETH

Much like claws, shed teeth can be used for protection and defensive magick. Shed baby teeth are great for protection charms for children. Teeth from animals have long been used in spells or charm bags to help relieve toothaches. Of course, this does not take the place of going to the dentist. The function of the tooth, especially sharp canine teeth, is to tear into something. This function will serve you well if a shed tooth is used in spells that are designed to "tear into something," meaning to really open something up to find what is hidden. Because teeth are bones, witches who "throw or read the bones" might choose to include them in their divination bag.

CAT WHISKERS

Cat whiskers are highly sensitive. Whiskers help cats find their way and give them feedback about tight spaces and obstacles, all while picking up on subtle energetic vibrations. Witches can use shed whiskers to "see in the dark." They show us how to make things fit and to see ways around any obstacles. Using shed whiskers for divination spells will add a huge boost. They will increase your sensitivity to energies and vibrations and improve your awareness. They can also be used for locator spells to find items that may be lost.

Cats, as high-vibrational beings, and especially familiars, travel frequently in the astral plane. Because whiskers help cats find their way and give them some level of security and protection, they are great to have on hand if you plan to travel into the astral realm. Cat whiskers are known for preventing nightmares as well. Place the shed whisker in a charm bag with lavender, chamomile, amethyst, and selenite to promote restful sleep and to keep the bad dreams away.

Whiskers are also known for being good luck charms in many cultures. Like wishing on an eyelash to manifest something, cat whiskers are powerful when it comes to manifestation magick. According to old witchcraft, you should whisper your wish into the whisker, and then burn it in the flame of a gold candle. Cat whiskers can be wonderful talismans for getting out of a fix and help prevent accidents, so keep shed whiskers in your car.

Cats were beloved by the Egyptian goddess Isis, the goddess of magick, who considered them to be personal mediums for her own power. Because of this, a cat's whiskers are revered as powerful catalysts for magickal workings. They will add power to any spell. Other uses for whiskers include help with agility, balance, and shedding old ways.

Ritual to Create a Charm Bag for Astral Travel

If you are planning on traveling into the astral realm or fear that you do so in your sleep, this sachet is an effective protection tool.

YOU WILL NEED

- Dried mugwort
- Dried valerian
- Dried rosemary
- Dried lavender
- Selenite
- Amethyst
- Shed cat whiskers
- Small natural-fiber bag that ties

DIRECTIONS

1. Put the dried herbs, crystals, and shed whiskers into the bag, hold it near your crown chakra, and intone the following:

   Into the astral I wish to go
   Please take me there without woe
   Whiskers guide and protect
   From the way home I will not defect.

2. Place the sachet under your pillow at night when you wish to travel into the astral realm or if you fear that you might travel.

TIP Shed fur, claws, teeth, and whiskers also make the purrfect offerings to deities such as Bast, Sekhmet, Freya, and Artemis.

THE MAGICK OF MEDITATING
⌒— WITH CATS —⌒

Those who practice meditation know of the benefits that it brings, from reducing stress and anxiety to improving memory and mood. When we involve our cats in this practice, we find unique advantages to having them near. For starters, they have an immediate calming effect on us. Many people report that they are able to clear their minds and reach the alpha state more quickly. You might notice that the color of the cat factors in during meditation as well, bringing those characteristics to the forefront so that you receive the messages aligned with them.

It is during meditation that we are often most open to receiving messages. Your feline familiar will sit with you, ensuring that the messages that need to be delivered come through and that you are receiving them in a way that you can understand. Don't be surprised if meditating with a cat ends up with a journey, be it into a past life or to another realm. Your cat will take you wherever you need to go and bring you back safely.

SPELLS THAT INCLUDE YOUR FAMILIAR
⌒— AND THEIR MAGICK —⌒

For the following spells, it is advised that you have your familiar with you in the room and, if possible, within your magickal circle. If your familiar has yet to come into physical form, remember that you can use the spell to call them to you. You can also call in a big cat familiar.

Each spell requires a candle of the color noted. Cast a protective circle before any of the workings and then call in your familiar. The candle should be placed on an altar or in your sacred space and lit before the spell is chanted. Each spell should be chanted at least three times unless you feel called to change that or your familiar advises differently. Remember to close the circle and thank your familiar for their assistance. Also, remember they appreciate offerings of cat treats, catnip, and, of course, salmon or tuna.

Spell for Protection

Do this spell when you want or need to have a little extra protection. Use a black candle.

> *Familiar, guardian lend me your power*
> *Protection is needed in this hour*
> *Our defenses we will raise*
> *Up around us the barrier stays*
> *Safe with my feline protector*
> *Until it is needed no more.*
> *As I will, so mote it be.*

Spell to Anchor for Astral Travel

Use this spell to anchor yourself in the physical realm while traveling in the astral plane. Use a purple candle.

> *An anchor I will need*
> *Feline familiar stay with me*
> *Keep me safe while I travel*
> *And bring my spirit back from the astral.*
> *So mote it be.*

Spell to Banish Negative Energies/Entities

Do this spell to expel any negative energies or entities around you or your home. Burn dried sage, rosemary, pine, or juniper in a fireproof dish just before intoning the spell. These herbs are all cleansing and protection herbs and will add a powerful boost to your spell as well as assisting in driving out the negative energies. Use a black candle.

As these herbs burn and smoke
My familiar's power I invoke
Feline guardian I call you to the ready
Entities dark and energies heavy
Negative spirits and unwanted guests
We banish you without protest!
As I will, so mote it be.

Spell to Cross Over a Lost/Trapped Soul

Do this spell when a soul needs to be crossed over to the other side. Use a white candle.

Lost or trapped, earthbound soul
The time has come for you to go
What ties you here abates
As familiar spirit guards the western gate
Crossing now with ease
May you finally be at peace.
So mote it be.

Spell to See Energy or Auras

Use this spell if you want or need to see different energies or auras. Use a dark blue or an indigo candle.

Feline familiar lend me your eyes
To look beyond the guise
The second sight please give to me
So that I may truly see
True vision is found
Now energies and auras abound.
So mote it be.

TIP ⟨ Remember to release this spell so that you are not constantly seeing *everything*. This can become quite overwhelming. The release will only take you back to whatever is normal for you, not obliterate your magickal sight completely. This is the spell to release:

Feline familiar I give you back your eyes
I have seen beyond the guise
The second sight is released from me
Now only what is normal to see
What was meant to be seen was found
Through the energies and auras around.
So mote it be.

Working with your familiar is a highly rewarding experience for both of you. You get the benefit of the additional power and magick that the feline can contribute and the familiar is fulfilling the oath to their witch as well as being in the presence of magick that is a bit like catnip to them. You both have the love and support of one another and that is often the biggest reward.

Cat Medicine

*Cats help us heal in ways that can be difficult
to comprehend. The medicine they offer us not only comes
in the form of healing, but also wisdom and knowledge.*

What is animal medicine? In its most pure, basic form, it is the essence of each animal that comes forth with lessons and healing for those who desire to listen and learn. The "medicine" is what we gain as the animal aids in helping to heal mind, body, and spirit.[12] These animal medicine teachings have been handed down through generations of Indigenous Peoples across the globe. Each Indigenous culture works with the animals that are relevant to their area. This does not mean that they cannot learn animal medicine from those in other regions and countries as well. Because animal medicine is strong and powerful, it is no wonder that witches, shamans, healers, and other magickal people seek to learn it and use it in their practices.

Much like the ancient Egyptians, Indigenous Peoples and shamans here in the Americas teach us that cats are to be revered, for they hold powerful magick and medicine. They teach us self-sufficiency and independence. They are known guardians of the spirit and bring good luck and good fortune. Their medicine brings with it the ability to remain poised and get our bearings. It also brings balance and the power to step boldly into our roles within our own life. Cat medicine teaches curiosity, mystery, playfulness, spontaneity, attentiveness, flexibility, and dexterity, and fosters the ability to stalk and hunt down that which we are seeking. It also teaches us patience and timing and to trust our intuition and instincts.

Mojave and Zuni peoples believed that the native wildcat spirit had healing properties and would help them on the hunt. The Pawnee people revere cat medicine as being associated with their ancestors and the stars. The fur of a wildcat was used as a protective garment.

In the Incan civilization, cat medicine helps identify heavier energies. This cat is typically the spirit of Otorongo, the sacred jaguar that comes from beyond the Rainbow Bridge and teaches the way of the luminous warrior. In the Quechua dialect spoken by Peruvian shamans, this heavy energy is called hucha. The feline spirit seeks out hucha and helps remove it from the energetic field and clear any blockages. Cat medicine also looks for the root cause of hucha, such as toxic relationships, childhood trauma, and possible imprints from past lives. As the cat curls itself around your energetic body, it helps you understand where this is coming from and will guide you in healing it.[13] One of the biggest mysteries of the cat is their power of transmutation. They hold the power to take heavy, dense feelings and energy and either get rid of it altogether or heal it.

Shamans believe that cat medicine also teaches us the language of love. They share with us what it means to set and maintain boundaries. They teach us what discipline means in relationships. Cats help us "deconstruct the socio-cultural conditioning of domination that we carry ingrained in the unconscious."[14] Cats help us break down these confines because of their independent and "I don't care what anyone says or thinks" attitude. They live in the moment and enjoy life rather than waiting to be told what to do or how to feel or act. People notice that even the most aloof cat comes to see what is going on in moments of great joy, as well as stay by their sides during moments of great sadness.

On her blog, Rose De Dan, shaman and Reiki master, recounts how her cat helped her Reiki practice by assisting with healing the clients as well as helping to heal herself, bridging the gap between humans and animals in the healing world.[15] This is what animal medicine does. It bridges the gap between humans and animals and the world of Spirit. We are often drawn to certain animals because we require their medicine and what they have to teach us about life.

⟜ FELINE POWER ANIMALS ⟞

When shamans talk about calling upon your power animal, this is the apex of their medicine. These are the greatest lessons and healing that an animal can offer you. A feline as a power animal won't ask you, they will tell you. They are more forceful in nature when compared to messengers and guides. If they are coming to you as a power animal, know that serious work is just around the corner. They will demand to be heard, but they will also guide you in what they are there to teach you and how to heal.

Because felines are so inherently connected to the world of Spirit, part of their medicine as a power animal is to bring you up to speed on all things mysterious and magickal. A cat power animal comes into play when you have forgotten your magick. They will show you why you are not embracing it and help you better understand it. They will remind you that *you are the magick*. For example, tiger power animals can show you how to live up to your greatest potential. Jaguar medicine improves your ability to see patterns in the chaos.

Feline power animals tell you to take a closer look. There are details that you are overlooking or missing. This medicine speaks to the "look before you leap" concept. They will show you how to dig deeper, to pierce the veil of mystery so that you may uncover what you need to know. Black panther power animals show you how to slip into the shadows to see into the beyond and how to boost your own psychic abilities. This power animal is a fierce ally for mothers who need help leaving a toxic environment or relationship. Cat medicine coming through a power animal gives us the ability to let go of codependency so that we can stand in our own power. They give us the courage and know-how to embrace change and become independent.

FELINE MEDICINE FOR
SPIRITUAL GROWTH

Our spiritual growth within each lifetime is what teaches and nurtures our soul. Our feline familiars come into our lives to help us in this regard. We can also use the medicine of the other felines for targeted spiritual development.

The first step is figuring out what your soul needs at the moment. This can come through asking your cat companion, guide, or familiar. You can also invoke big cat energy and ask whoever shows up what you should be addressing. Remember, there are a multitude of cat deities that can be called upon for advice, knowledge, and assistance.

A simple spell invoking feline energy may help you find the answer. Once you have the information, a ritual can be performed to utilize this knowledge and the cat medicine that aligns with it.

Meditation Work to Seek Spiritual Growth

When going into a meditation, it is important to be able to be still and quiet. You will need to be in a comfortable place that allows for this. Make sure you're not hungry, thirsty, or need to go to the restroom. Closing your eyes helps so that you can relax your body and your mind. Calm your breathing (usually three to six deep breaths in and out) and clear your mind. If any errant thoughts intrude, simply let them float away so that the messages from your higher self, familiar, guides, angels, Deity, or the Universe can come through. Use the following meditation work to find what your soul needs for spiritual growth.

YOU WILL NEED

- Comfortable place to sit where you will not be disturbed
- Purple candle
- Cauldron or fireproof dish
- 1 teaspoon dried mugwort
- Lighter
- 1 tablespoon clear alcohol to help herbs burn (Everclear burns cleanest without extra smoke or smell)
- Timer
- Journal and pen

DIRECTIONS

1. Place the candle, cauldron, and mugwort on your altar or in your sacred space and take a seat.
2. Cast a circle.
3. Light the purple candle.
4. Pour the alcohol into the cauldron.
5. Sprinkle in the mugwort, light it with the lighter, and let burn. (Note: Be careful when working with fire, taking the necessary precautions.)

6. Intone the following:

> *Cat medicine for spiritual growth*
> *Guide me and give your oath*
> *To show me what I must address*
> *Help to gain knowledge without duress*
> *Let me see what my soul is seeking*
> *I pledge to listen while you are speaking.*

7. Set the timer for ten to fifteen minutes.
8. Close your eyes and begin the meditation.
9. Once the timer goes off, ground and center yourself.
10. Write down any messages you received, particularly regarding what needs to be done for your soul growth.
11. Open the circle.

NOTE ⟨ Make sure all fire is out.

WORKING RITUALS FOR SOUL GROWTH
⟶ WITH FELINE MEDICINE ⟵

Once you know what you need to work on, you can decide how to go about it. One way to do that is through ritual. Since most felines harbor lunar energy, working with the phases of the Moon is often appropriate. The New Moon is perfect for setting intentions. The Waxing Moon phases help fulfill the intentions that were set on the New Moon. Full Moon energy is wonderful for releasing and clearing out what is no longer serving us. Waning Moon phases lend power for banishing. Days of the week also correspond to different energies (see page 138). In these aspects, cat medicine shows us how timing can affect our plan of action.

Use the knowledge you have gained in the previous chapters regarding the energy of cats in general as well as guides, familiars, big cats, and power animals to assess which one will be most effective for your ritual work. For example, if part of your spiritual work is to become a better leader and grow your communication skills, working with lion medicine on a Wednesday (the day of Mercury for communication) would be most effective. Should you need to do deep shadow work around your codependency, call for black panther medicine on either a Saturday (for banishing) or a Tuesday (for action). Is your magick part of how you need to grow spiritually? Ask your familiar or feline companion for their medicine to help you in a working best performed on a Monday. To see which magickal tools match with your ritual work, see page 138 for different tools and their meanings.

FELINE MEDICINE FOR SPIRITUAL
AND EMOTIONAL HEALING

One of the bravest things we can do is dive into our spiritual and emotional healing. Many times we have spiritual or energetic issues going on that begin to manifest as physical issues within our bodies. When we begin to take control of our spiritual and emotional well-being, it has a ripple effect throughout our bodies and then our lives. We see the positive effects of our personal healing in our home, our relationships, and how we function in society.

Invoking the medicine that the cat has to offer for healing will be a powerful ally for you. Remember that cat medicine helps us:

- Clear out heavy energies
- Set and maintain healthy boundaries
- Balance work and play
- Be Zen masters
- Cast out self-doubt and trust ourselves, our intuition, and our instincts

Sometimes we need to call upon cat medicine; other times it shows up for us through messages and guides. Be open to what is showing up for you.

Remember that healing work can be difficult, so be gentle with yourself. Be aware of what is coming up for you over the next few weeks. You can continue to light a white candle every week and intone the chant three times until you feel that it has taken hold.

If you are doing healing work for others, this spell is easy to apply to them as well.

Ritual for Healing with Cat Medicine

Use this ritual to invoke cat medicine for healing.

- Comfortable place to sit where you will not be disturbed
- White cat candle
  (a regular white candle will do
  if a cat candle cannot be found,
  as white is the color of healing)
- Cauldron or fireproof dish
- 1-2 small pieces of paper and a pen
- Lighter or matches

DIRECTIONS

1. Find a comfortable place to sit where you will not be disturbed, such as your sacred space.
2. Set the white cat candle and the cauldron on your altar.
3. Cast a circle.
4. Write on a strip of paper what needs to be healed (keep to one or two things at a time so as not to be overwhelmed).
5. Light your candle and intone the following once:

Feline medicine I call to you
We have this work to do
Healing energy is what I need
Bring to me with gentle speed
Whether mind, body, or spirit
Cat medicine come here to heal it.
So mote it be (after the third time).

6. Say out loud what is written on the paper.
7. Light the paper and drop it into the cauldron.
8. Say the chant twice more (for a total of three times).
9. If any cat in particular showed up for you, thank them for their assistance.

10. Make sure the paper burns up completely. As always, be careful when working with open flames.

11. Open the circle.

12. Dispose of the spell ash off of your property to ensure that what was plaguing you is not lingering in your space.

NOTE ⟨ Do not trespass on private property to dispose of spell remains. Burying the ash is the preferred method as the Earth's energy can easily absorb this and transmute it. If this is not possible, it is acceptable to place the spell remains in a garbage receptacle.

RITUAL WORK WITH HEALING
⸺ CAT MEDICINE ⸺

The healing spell on the opposite page can also be incorporated into ritual work, again taking the Moon phases and days of the week into consideration. Because rituals tend to be longer than a quick circle cast and incantation, they aren't something you would want to do in a pinch. However, they can be a wonderful option for deep-seated issues that may need a little more work. This can be true of trauma and issues surrounding familial or societal conditioning.

Invoking cat medicine into your ritual work is a beautiful and very personal thing. For rituals, you might consider calling upon one of the cat deities (discussed in 'A Being Worthy of the Gods') along with a feline power animal that aligns with the healing work being done (see 'Big Cat Energy' for the list of big cats). This will offer a powerful combination of feline energy and medicine.

The lunar ties of the majority of the felines may bring up strong emotional aspects when calling upon them during a ritual. This is okay. This simply means that there is work to be done there and that the healing is beginning to take place. After all, the first step in healing is acknowledging that there is an issue. Cat medicine will allow you to feel these emotions, learn where they come from, and help you address them in the most effective way. Be aware, though, that sometimes cat medicine is not as gentle as we would like it to be. Sometimes healing means ripping off the bandage and examining the wound. Being in ritual with feline medicine can leave you feeling raw and exposed, but it will not abandon you to yourself. Cat medicine energy will stay with you as long as you need it for continued healing.

THE HEALING POWER OF THE HOUSE CAT

Our little balls of fur have plenty of medicine to offer all on their own. They are the ultimate Zen masters. They live utterly in the moment, eating when they're hungry, sleeping when they're tired, and playing whenever the urge arises.

Cats know when their human needs healing. How often have you had a rough day at work and once you're home, your cat is winding around your leg and acting extra needy? They are acknowledging that they feel your stress. This simple touch is the cat sharing their auric field with you. Once you sit down and try to relax, they climb onto your chest and start to purr. They are now sharing the stress-relieving and healing vibration that a cat's purr holds.

The Power of the Purr

According to an article in *Scientific American*, cats not only purr when they are happy and content, but also while they are under duress. Why? Well, as many in sound therapy know, there is a range of frequencies that promote healing and well-being. A cat's purr ranges from 25 to 150 Hertz, a frequency range that has been shown to improve bone density, promote muscle and tissue health, and boost overall healing.[16] This frequency is also known to help heal broken bones, improve joint health, and facilitate wound healing.[16]

If you experience dyspnea or shortness of breath, a cat's purr may help with this. Some studies have shown that a patient with chronic obstructive pulmonary disease (COPD) benefits by having a purring feline sit on their chest. The longer the cat is willing to sit there and purr, the more relief the COPD patient receives.[17] Studies also show that a cat's purr can effectively reduce blood pressure and stress. Because the healing frequency can help repair tissue damage and lower blood pressure, otherwise healthy cat adoptees have a 40 percent less risk of heart attack than those without a cat.[17]

Anti-Anxiety Cat Healing

The cat's purr is a natural anti-anxiety pill. But wait, there's more. The simple act of petting a cat releases oxytocin, which is the "feel good" hormone. The release of oxytocin reduces stress and anxiety. Some people find that their breathing patterns change while sitting with a cat. They can become unconsciously synchronized and bring on a state of meditative coherence. This in and of itself is mindfulness, compassion, kindness, and love that all come from the heart.

Our feline friends are highly attuned to geopathic energies, the flow of vibrational patterns and disruptions from the Earth. When there are areas of highly concentrated disruptions, it causes geopathic stress. When humans live in these areas, they can begin to manifest physical symptoms. Studies conducted by geobiologists nearly a century ago show that geopathic stress has been shown to affect our natural ability to recharge and self-heal because it can cause insomnia, extreme anxiety, and poor health. In children it can manifest as sleepwalking and persistent bedwetting issues.[18]

Cats act as buffers for these geopathic areas. Because of their vibrational frequency and ability to transmute heavy energies, cats are unbothered by geopathic stress. In fact, they seek out these areas to sit in, which may seem odd to you. If you live in a geopathic zone (you can search your area to find out), it is likely your cat purposefully goes to the most heavily concentrated areas to transmute the unhealthy energy or to break it up altogether. Even while we are unaware, our cats are looking out for us.

Magickal Tools

In this section you will find information on magickal days of the week, Moon and Sun phases/timing, candle magick and corresponding colors, as well as some basic herbs and crystals. All of these things can be used alongside your familiar's power to strengthen spells as well as bring your magickal workings to the next level. For example, if you are working a protection spell using a black candle dressed with (common) sage and rosemary and perform it on a Saturday, the magick tied to it is some of the most powerful available. If you want to try a communication spell with your familiar, work it on a Wednesday using a blue candle.

⌑—— MAGICKAL DAYS OF THE WEEK ——⌑

Each day of the week holds a specific energy. When we align our magickal workings with the day that corresponds with what we are trying to achieve, it reinforces the intentions of the spell and adds power.

Sunday: The Sun's Day: Divine Masculine, success, happiness, joy, vitality, creativity, confidence

Monday: The Moon's Day: Dreams, the subconscious, intuition, scrying, divination, water magick, emotions, women's magick, domestic issues

Tuesday: Mars's Day: Quick action, ambition, sexual potency, passion, personal strength, self-assertion, victory, protection

Wednesday: Mercury's Day: Communication, technology, focus and alertness, learning, writing

Thursday: Jupiter's Day: Luck, abundance and prosperity, increasing and preserving wealth, business

Friday: Venus's Day: Divine Feminine, love, relationships and friendships, beauty, glamour magick, peace and harmony

Saturday: Saturn's Day: Protection, banishing and binding, communing with ancestors and departed spirits, overcoming obstacles

MOON PHASES

As witches, we are well aware of the powerful energies that the Moon holds. When we align our spells with the different Moon phases, it will further empower them with the energy of that phase. Because most of our feline familiar's energy naturally syncs with the Moon, they can easily facilitate a deeper working for you.

 New or Dark Moon: Setting intentions, manifesting, new beginnings, shadow work

 Waxing Crescent: Nurturing, self-love, compassion, courage, positive mind-set

First Quarter: Drawing things to you such as a new job, love interest, success, money, etc.

 Waxing Gibbous: Fertility, endurance, breaking through what one may be resisting

 Full Moon: Release, letting go of what no longer serves us, cleansing, protection

 Waning Gibbous: Minor banishings, cleansing

 Last Quarter: Removing obstacles, allowing flow with ease, breaking addictions

 Waning Crescent: Major banishings, removing toxic relationships or situations

⟡— SUN TIMING —⟡

The Sun also holds its own powerful energies and we can use specific timing throughout the day to aid our spell and ritual work. You can also connect with solar feline energies such as the lion or the Egyptian deity Sekhmet to help facilitate Sun magick into your workings.

Sunrise/Dawn: New beginnings, manifestation, hope, charging energies

Morning: Growth, building, relationships, wealth

Noon: Protection, justice, health, courage, success

Afternoon: Clarity, resolution, business communication

Sunset: Endings, release/letting go, banishment, divination

⸎ CANDLE MAGICK ⸎

Candles are commonplace materials when it comes to rituals and spell work. Witches use them on altars and to create sacred space, cast circles, and more. Using various candle colors for a working can be an extremely effective way to boost the spell's power. Like most other things in witchcraft, candles hold their own vibrational patterns and the different colors align with specific magickal workings.

When working with candles, you may decide to "dress" it to increase the potency of your magick. Dressing a candle includes the use of oils and herbs. Typically, a carrier oil is used (an oil that is paired with essential oils to dilute them, such as jojoba, sweet almond, or even olive oil) to anoint the candle. This is simply rubbing the candle with the oil and giving it its purpose through stating the intentions of the working. The anointed candle is then rolled in dried herbs that correspond with the spell.

Use the following candle correspondences to manifest your magickal intentions.

 White (can be used in place of any other color): Healing, spirituality, peace, purity

 Black: Protection, banishing, binding, repelling negative energies, magick (also associated with witches)

 Brown: Earth energy (grounding), animals, stability, home protection, family

Red: Vitality, passion, romantic love, strength, fast action, courage, root chakra

Pink: Self-love, friendship, emotional healing, nurturing

Yellow: Happiness, joy, success, power, Sun energy, solar plexus chakra

 Orange: Creativity, expression, adventure, positivity, sacral chakra

Green: Nature, physical healing, money (abundance and prosperity), growth, heart chakra

Blue: Communication, inspiration, calming, throat (royal blue) and third eye (indigo) chakras

Purple: Psychic abilities, hidden knowledge, divination, astral projection, crown chakra

Silver: Divine Feminine, intuition, dreams, Moon energies

Gold: Divine Masculine, wealth, luck, happiness, Sun energies

MAGICKAL HERBS

All plants have unique vibrational patterns and properties. Many of them have strong magickal energies as well as medicinal uses. The list of magickal plants is almost endless, so we'll just cover some of the basics here.

 Healing: Angelica, yarrow, echinacea, lemon balm, tansy, rosemary, horehound

 Protection: Sage, rosemary, pine, juniper, cedar, garlic, rue, nettles, angelica

Communication: Clary sage, rosemary, bay leaf

 Love: Red (romance) and pink (self and friends) roses, lavender, vanilla, basil, jasmine

 Money: Basil, cinnamon, bay leaf, mint, juniper, cinquefoil, alfalfa

 Divination: Mugwort, rosemary, clary sage, dandelion, star anise

Calming/sleep: Lavender, chamomile, lemon balm, bergamot, St. John's wort

Fertility: Pine and spruce (to balance masculine and feminine), cinnamon, nettles, vanilla, willow, red and orange roses petals (to activate root and sacral chakras/sex organs)

Happiness and joy: Marjoram, lavender, St. John's wort, mint, lemon balm, pine

 Divine Feminine: Spruce, willow, motherwort, jasmine, mugwort, apple

 Divine Masculine: Pine, sunflower, mint, bay leaf, basil, St. John's wort, oak leaves

⌘ AURAS ⌘

Auras are invisible energy fields that surround everything and everyone and are part of a more complex system called the subtle energy body. There are seven layers to the human aura, each connected to our overall health. Auras can be different colors, and each color is associated with its own meaning. Below is a quick list of some of the main aura colors and their meanings. Please note that auras are a much more complex subject of magick work; this is just a simple guide to get you started.

- **Red:** Well grounded, passionate, strong-minded
- **Orange:** Adventurous, active, considerate
- **Yellow:** Positive, creative, open-minded
- **Green:** Kind, compassionate, communicator
- **Blue:** Intuitive, peaceful, spiritual
- **Indigo:** Sensitive, curious, inner knowing
- **Violet:** Inquisitive, intelligent, connected to spirit world

CRYSTAL CORRESPONDENCES

Crystals are powerful magickal allies. They boost our own energies and that of the spell. They protect, help heal, and facilitate communication between our higher selves, the Universe, Deity, and our guides. We can charge them for a specific purpose and carry them as a talisman or use them to create grids. Combining their energy with other magickal tools, such as herbs or candle magick and the energy that your familiar can and will lend to you will further empower your workings.

Crystals can be added to mojo or charm bags along with herbs and other magickal items for a variety of uses, including protection, sleep, money drawing, and healing. You can also create a grid with crystals for these same purposes. Crystal grids use the power of sacred geometry to combine the energy of the individual crystals you are using for a specific working. Crystal grid layouts can easily be found online. For example, if you want to create a powerful grid for protection, you could use the above listed protection crystals along with some sage and rosemary. Include some shed cat claws for an added boost. You can ask your familiar to infuse their natural protective instincts into the grid.

When we use all of our magickal knowledge and incorporate tools such as magickal timing (days of the week, Moon or Sun phases), candle color correspondences, or herbs and crystals, it take less energy from ourselves to work the spell and requires less energy from our familiar. Using this wisdom to aid you gives the needed boost without tapping into your own precious well of energy that is often required for the higher and more complex magicks.

 Healing: Amethyst, clear quartz, bloodstone, lepidolite, labradorite, agate, sugilite

 Protection: Black obsidian, black tourmaline, smoky quartz, labradorite, jet

 Communication: Sodalite, petalite, fluorite, blue lace agate

 Love: Rose quartz, garnet, ruby, rhodochrosite, rhodonite

 Money: Jade, pyrite, goldstone, emerald, citrine, tiger's eye

 Divination: Selenite, moonstone, labradorite, petalite, lapis lazuli

 Calming/sleep: Amethyst, selenite, moonstone, aquamarine, bloodstone

 Fertility: Pink tourmaline, red/orange carnelian, moonstone, garnet, green aventurine

Happiness and joy: Citrine, sunstone, dalmatian jasper, tiger's eye

The Tail End

It is hard to put into words how important the existence of feline energy really is. These magickal creatures do more for us than we can imagine. They are so much greater than just our companions. There are those who say they are strictly dog people until a purring cat in their lap has them completely enthralled.

Feline energy is powerful and healing. It is gentle and reassuring but also harsh and unforgiving when necessary. It is independence. It is curiosity and a sense of adventure. It is bravery and the willingness to fight for what is rightfully yours. It is self-confidence and leadership. It is bringing our whole self forward unapologetically. It's the shadows and the light. It's magick and mystery.

The essence of a cat's energy alone would be enough for their veneration across the globe. Many civilizations and cultures saw and felt this, but also recognized the magick that lies at the core of each feline. When cats chose to work alongside humans, the ancients acknowledged that these special creatures knew more than they did on a spiritual, energetic, and magickal level. They allied the cats for their workings and the healing medicine they could offer, creating a mutually beneficial relationship.

The stories of cat magick were passed down through the ages, reaching witches, shamans, and healers. Magickal people continued working with felines, often bringing about their own demise, particularly during medieval times when women and witches were persecuted by the Church. While the Church feared cats for the magick they held, and persecuted them alongside accused witches, the resilient spirit of the cat refused to give up and forsake us. This speaks to their innate sense of loyalty.

A cat's connection to the spirit world is virtually unparalleled, acting as a messenger and guide for their humans. The auric field and vibrational frequency of cats helps us connect to the realm of Spirit on a deeper level. When a familiar spirit chooses a witch and manifests in the physical form of a cat, their magickal power is unrivaled by any other animal. They teach us, lend us power and magick, deliver messages, stand as a guardian and protector, and come to our aid for spiritual growth and healing.

Working with the energy and magick of a feline is of great benefit to us. It can open doors and show us things we might never have thought to question. Even if you do not or cannot have a cat, you can still work with these energies using the techniques and spells found here in this book. Feline energy can be invoked, whether it is the domestic cat or that of a big cat. We can call upon feline animal guides and power animals. I have learned that as a magickal being, our covenant with Spirit is that when we call, they show up, and that when they call to us, we should also feel compelled to show up and listen to what needs to be heard or tended to. More often than not, cat energy tells us that we need to show up for ourselves in ways that we haven't before.

These magickal little creatures made their way into our lives several millennia ago. It has been said that they have bewitched us. Perhaps there is some truth in this. If there is, then we are the ones benefiting from the magick of the cat.

Thank You

I would like to thank my best friend, my twin flame, and the sister of my soul, Coley. Thank you for giving me the courage to live my authentic life and find out who I truly am. Thank you for your love, your support, and for always being there for me. Thank you for sharing the laughs, the tears, and the adventures on and off the trail.

A huge thank you to my clan and coven sisters. Lady Lumosulo and Lady Eala, you were with me throughout this journey and helped me to believe in myself so that I could manifest this amazing opportunity. Thank you for your love and support.

About the Author

RIEKA MOONSONG is a Wiccan High Priestess who is currently training to become clergy. She is also an Andean tradition-trained, mesa-carrying shaman. It is her journey, soul path, and goddess-given gift to teach, to share wisdom and knowledge with others, and to help facilitate healing and growth for those on their own journey. She resides in Colorado with her feline familiar, Artemis.

Rieka has always felt the call to work with animals and their energies, even as a child. She currently has twenty-one animal guides and uses her natural ability to connect with them for wisdom and guidance. It is her dream to help others form close bonds with their familiars as well as other animals, and to teach them how to call upon these energies when they are needed. *Cat Magick* is a true labor of love for her.

References

1. Wikipedia, "Cats in Ancient Egypt." https://en.wikipedia.org/wiki/Cats_in_ancient_Egypt.

2. Worldbook.com, "Mythic Monday: The Riddle of the Sphinx." https://www.worldbook.com/behind-the-headlines/Mythic-Monday-The-Riddle-of-the-Sphinx.

3. Rucha Vijay Bodas, "Cats in Chinese Art," DailyArtMagazine.com, November 27, 2022. https://www.dailyartmagazine.com/cats-in-chinese-art.

4. Marie Kitsunebi, "Cat Yōkai! All 5 Kinds of Supernatural Cats from Japanese Folklore," Yōkai Street, September 21, 2020. https://www.yōkaistreet.com/cat-yōkai-all-5-kinds-of-supernatural-cats-from-japanese-folklore.

5. La Vocelle, "History of the Cat in the Dark Ages (Part 1)," TheGreatCat.org, November 23, 2012, by https://www.thegreatcat.org/history-of-the-cat-in-the-dark-ages-part-1.

6. Frances Simpson, *The Book of the Cat* (Whitefish, MT: Kessinger Publishing, 1903, 2010).

7. Irina Metzler, "Heretical Cats: Animal Symbolism in Religious Discourse," *Medium Aevum Quotidianum* 59 (2009): 16–33.

8. Wikipedia, "Cat Lady." https://en.wikipedia.org/wiki/Cat_lady.

9. Elena Harris, "Cat Spirit Animal," SpiritAnimalInfo.com. https://www.spiritanimal.info/cat-spirit-animal.

10. "The Energetic Power of Cats and Their Spiritual Meaning,"

LittleMissCat.com. https://littlemisscat.com/the-energetic-power-of-cats-and-their-spiritual-meaning.

11. Cherokee Billie, "Cats Superpowers Protect You from Negative Forces," CherokeeBillieSpiritualAdvisor.com, July 8, 2018. https://cherokeebilliespiritualadvisor.com/blogs/all/cats-superpowers-protect-you-from-negative-forces.

12. R. Kayne, "What Is Native American Animal Medicine?" LanguageHumanities.org, September 28, 2022. https://www.languagehumanities.org/what-is-native-american-animal-medicine.htm.

13. "Shamanic Medicine," Cat-Faith.com. https://www.cat-faith.com/isdoing/shamanichealing.

14. Yoskhaz, "The Medicine of the Cat," Institutoyoskhaz.com, March 21, 2022. https://institutoyoskhaz.com/uncategorized-en/the-medicine-of-the-cat.

15. Rose De Dan, "Shaman: Feline Healer and Teacher," ReikiShamanic.com, November 22, 2012. https://reikishamanic.com/2012/11/22/shaman-feline-healer-and-teacher.

16. Leslie A. Lyons, "Why Do Cats Purr?" *Scientific American*, April 3, 2006. https://www.scientificamerican.com/article/why-do-cats-purr/?gclid=Cj0KCQiA7bucBhCeARIsAIOwr-9LLCw8_cU2AuvEofjLMvx_vo6LyYPBJ5mY9UKppoNJTf2BPoTxhl0aAtPqEALw_wcB.

17. Broad, Michael. "Does the Cat's Purr Help Alleviate Symptoms of Dyspnoea in Humans?" PoC. PoC, February 27, 2022. https://pictures-of-cats.org/does-the-cats-purr-help-alleviate-symptoms-of-dyspnoea-in-humans.html.

18. Cerrano, Laura. "What Is Geopathic Stress?" LinkedIn, April 23, 2021. https://www.linkedin.com/pulse/what-geopathic-stress-laura-cerrano-/.

Index